Super Prestige Chester

Michael Yelton

© 2023 Michael Yelton and MDS Book Sales

ISBN 9781905304974

Contents

Photo Credits

BCVM	British Commercial Vehicle Museum	STA	Senior Transport Archive
HSPC	Harry Postlethwaite collection	TL/HH	Transport Library, Harry Hay
JAS	John A Senior	TL/PH	Transport Library. Peter Henson
MTMS	MTMS archive - Bob Hill collection	TL/RM	Transport Library, Roy Marshall
OS	Omnibus Society		

Front Cover
The first of the 1950 repeat order for Massey bodied Fodens was 77, which was here bound for the General Station. *(TL/PH)*

Outside Rear Cover
Tramcar No 3 seen at the Cross just about to head down Bridge Street with the famous Rows in the background. *(MTMS)*

1: INTRODUCTION

Transport in the City of Chester in some respects followed a conventional course. Initially street transport was provided by horse trams operated by a private company, but in January 1902 the Council took over the system under the powers of compulsory purchase which had been given to it under the terms of the Tramways Act 1870. The City Council was given the power under its own Act, passed in 1901, to run the services but also to convert them to electric power. It did this and also extended the small system, but the coverage of the city remained somewhat restricted in its extent.

A serious proposal by the Corporation to run buses emerged as early as 1906, and it was decided to purchase three vehicles to start services to areas which the trams did not serve. However, the following year a Special Meeting of the Council reversed this decision and the scheme did not proceed. This would have been a very early date for the commencement of a municipal bus service; it also would have pre-empted the development by other operators, and particularly Crosville, based in the city, of local services.

Once the City Council had made that decision, and despite a number of subsequent flirtations with the idea of running buses, it was 1928 before the decision was made not only to run motor vehicles, but also to abandon the tramways. As with many smaller systems, modernisation was badly needed by this time and the capital expenditure which was required to do that was disproportionate to the revenue to be expected.

The Chester Corporation Act 1928 gave the Council the powers which it required to run buses and on 12 February 1930 these began, replacing the trams in one fell swoop.

Because of the delays which had occurred, Crosville had commenced a number of local services and the way in which the Road Traffic Act 1930 was in practice operated by the Traffic Commissioners protected existing services. In 1932 the Council and Crosville entered into an important agreement, after which they exchanged some services, but also agreed spheres of influence within the city; the Council essentially agreed not to serve a portion of their ratepayers.

Chester had always been a compact settlement and this only began to change during and after the Second World War. The hostilities saw the construction of a number of camps for the armed forces on the outskirts, which resulted in a great deal of extra traffic. After the War, the city began expanding, particularly on the north side and there was a great deal of development both in the sector which had been allocated to Crosville under the 1932 agreement and, further west, in Blacon, which had been allocated to Chester and through which they had taken over a former Crosville service. In 1954 Chester absorbed what had been the former Urban District of Hoole, in which Crosville had established many local services.

The immediate post-war period saw a substantial increase in the fleet and the purchase of a variety of vehicles, including a number of Fodens, which were manufactured in Sandbach, within the County of Cheshire. However, the usual factors which adversely affected passenger numbers existed here and were combined with very severe traffic congestion, which made services unreliable. The local government changes of 1974 had little effect in this area and the Council continued in the same vein, until deregulation and the need to establish an arm's length company irrevocably affected the operations.

These themes are discussed in more detail later. Little has been written previously on Chester's operation, but the Manchester Transport Museum Society published as long ago as 1979 a now long out of print book by WD Clark and HG Dibdin. David Clark was then the manager of the municipal operation. That did not purport to be a full history, but has provided a great deal of information. Then in 2002 Ron Phillips wrote a short history to mark the centenary of the commencement of the municipal electric tramway, which was published by the City Council's stand-alone bus operating company. Nevertheless, for this book, the facts have been checked against the minutes of the Transport Committee to ensure that the information given is as accurate as possible.

2: BACKGROUND

Chester was, as its name implies, a foundation of the Romans. Chester comes from the Latin word castra, meaning a camp or garrison: the settlement was founded in 79AD under the name Deva Victrix. It then developed into a major civilian settlement, with a large amphitheatre, and continued to grow as such after the Romans left. The Romans set out the basic street pattern in the centre of the town, and the four main ways met at The Cross, the effective centre of the city.

In 689 King Aethelred of Mercia founded a Minster church in Chester, which later became the first cathedral. It was in due course superseded by the present cathedral, which again is in the centre of the old town and which contains a great deal of Norman work, much altered over the years. When the Normans invaded, Chester was one of the last towns to fall to them, and after his rule had been fully established William the Conqueror ordered that a castle should be constructed there, to control the access to North Wales. The castle became of great importance in the various campaigns against the Welsh in the early years of the Middle Ages.

Town walls were constructed around the mediaeval town, as they were in many places, but here they have remained largely complete and still encircle the centre of the town, or city as it became in 1541. Many buildings from the Middle Ages remain in the centre, and they were added to during the Victorian period, when the use of quasi-mediaeval black and white became fashionable. The unique feature of Chester's architecture are the Rows, which consist of shops and houses on two storeys, with a continuous walkway at first floor level. Horse racing began very early and the racecourse, which has been used ever since, is unusually close to the city centre and near the river.

The Industrial Revolution and the coming of the railway gave a new impetus to Chester. The River Dee was once more important than the Mersey for commerce, but has been silting up since the Middle Ages and thus Chester did not develop as a port, although canals were constructed. Chester General station opened in 1848 and became an important centre for trains to London via Crewe and also to North Wales and Holyhead (for Ireland). The station was

A horse bus awaits passengers in the Market Place. *(MTMS)*

4

constructed some distance out of the city centre, as happened in Oxford, Cambridge and other places with fine architecture in the commercial heart; this had a very substantial effect on the development of the local transport infrastructure, as there was a continuing need to carry passengers from the station into the shopping and business area. The horse tramway depot was established in close proximity to the station, and in turn that became the electric tram depot and then the bus garage for the City Council.

A second station, Northgate, opened in 1875 as a terminus for the Cheshire Lines Committee. It was never as important as General, although it was nearer to the city centre, and it closed in 1969 and was demolished.

The very large Town Hall was opened in 1869 and built in a Gothic Revival style. In due course Chester was designated as a County Borough, a status which reflected its historic importance and its place in local life rather than its still small population.

The major landowners in the city have been the Grosvenor family, Dukes of Westminster; their seat is at Eaton Hall, near Eccleston, just to the south of the city. The Grosvenor estates strongly influenced the development of Chester, especially in the later Victorian age. Their name is perpetuated in many buildings and areas of the city.

The boundary of the Chester local authority was quite restricted and some of the villages outside it became quite large; some were in time served by the local authority Transport Undertaking. This tendency was particularly marked on the south-west side, where the village of Saltney grew very substantially. Saltney was, however, in Flintshire, and thus in Wales, and it would have been particularly politically sensitive to extend the city boundary in that direction. The trams did not cross the boundary, although on electrification the terminus was very near to the national line, but a low railway bridge blocked access. In 1932 Chester began running its buses into Saltney itself and thus established a unique position for itself; no other municipality ran from England into Wales. There was also an area not far behind the General Station which formed the separate Urban District of Hoole, and this was to be of some importance later in the way in which local transport developed. Blacon, which developed after the War into one of the largest council estates in Europe, was originally in a separate parish known as Blacon cum Crabwall until 1 April 1936, when it was incorporated into Chester.

Chester has always had many contacts with North Wales and for many years the more serious criminal cases from that area were tried in the

The boundary, and the offending railway bridge. *(MTMS)*

city. The Welsh for Chester is Caer and that can now be seen on the bilingual destination blinds carried by some services running in from Wrexham and around.

After the Second World War there was severe pressure on land use in Chester as more housing was needed. This was concentrated on the northern side of the city, partly in the north-eastern area of Newton by Chester, which had been allocated to Crosville under the 1932 agreement, but partly in the north-western sector, which had been given to the City Council under that understanding. The new estate of Blacon was constructed there over many years, partly on a former Army camp, and provided the city with its most frequent and lucrative services, albeit of considerable and sometimes bewildering complexity. The newly developed areas, however, as with those already built, were largely flat and did not require more powerful vehicles.

The nature of the street pattern in the centre, coupled with the growth of private motoring, led to traffic congestion which was even worse than in many similar towns and had an adverse effect on the reliability and speed of the local bus services. New traffic schemes began to be introduced, including the construction of an Inner Ring Road, and then the commencement of bus priority schemes in the area within the walls. New roads were also opened around the town, so that the very heavy traffic to the resorts on the North Wales coast was taken out of the city. However, tourism became a more important factor in the economy of the city and this meant more visitors and thus congestion.

It cannot be emphasised, however, that even with the growth, Chester has remained a small city. As late as 2011, by which time it had been subsumed into the Cheshire West and Chester unitary authority, the population of the Chester area, the former City, was still just less than 80,000. Apart from tourism, there are a substantial number of service companies in Chester, and it also acts as a dormitory for Liverpool, to which there are frequent train services.

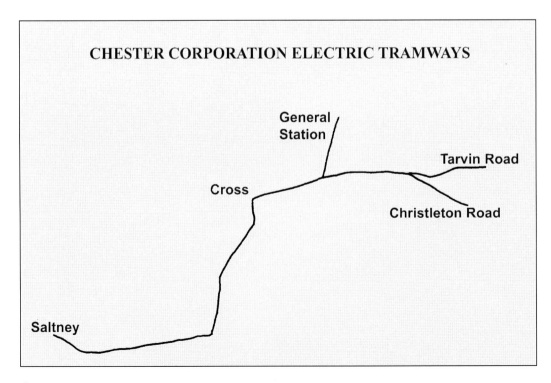

CHESTER CORPORATION ELECTRIC TRAMWAYS

3: THE TRAMWAYS OF CHESTER

The need for public transport in Chester was to a considerable extent driven by the fact that the main railway station was so far from the centre of the city. Indeed, when it was opened a new street, City Road, was also constructed to join the station to the existing road to the east from the Cross and this itself rapidly became filled with hotels, shops and the like. There were hackney carriages for hire, but they were by their nature restricted to the better off. As early as 1870 one W Hewitt started a horse bus service from the Town Hall to the Station, but it could carry only about 12 passengers and luggage. The Grosvenor Hotel in Eastgate Street, one of the largest in the area, also had their own small horse bus at this time, for its patrons.

In 1877 the manager of the Liverpool horse tramways, T Lloyd, visited Chester and rapidly became enthused by the idea of a line connecting the station to the city centre, and then on to the growing suburb of Saltney. Public meetings were organised and a great deal of interest was shown: the Chester Tramways Company was set up, and the capital was subscribed with some alacrity. Operations were authorised by the Chester Tramways Act 1878, which was passed on 22 July of that year.

The company was given permission to construct two lines, which abutted on to each other and were, in fact, run as one. The first was from Grosvenor Road, just short of the Grosvenor toll bridge over the Dee, through the centre, serving the Cross, then east along Eastgate and Foregate Streets, followed by a turn north into City Road and thus up to the station. The second continued from Grosvenor Road, over the bridge, and then turning due west along Hough Green and Chester Street to terminate at the junction with Curzon Street. This was shortly before the railway bridge carrying a line across the road, near Saltney Station, and a few hundred yards short of the boundary with Wales, which was on the far side of the railway line. The problem with this line was that while Saltney was a destination which would provide traffic, there was little building on the Grosvenor Bridge route (as opposed to the alternative, much narrower, Dee Bridge), and the Hough Green area had only a number of large houses which were unlikely to provide many passengers.

Construction proceeded with some expedition and the official opening was on 10 June 1879. An important decision was taken at that time to site the operation on land which was acquired for that purpose from the London and North Western Railway Company, and which was very near to the original passenger terminal in Chester, which had been converted to a goods and repair depot once the General Station was in operation. This long-lasting site was very well situated: it was not far from the centre of town, and adjacent to one of the important termini. A house was also constructed on the site for the manager. The gauge was the standard, of 4 feet 8½ inches, and the line was single-track with passing loops; the exact position of all of these is not clear.

Operations began on a 10-minute frequency during the day, with eight Eades Patent Reversible cars, which were small double-deckers which required two horses. It was very soon appreciated that these were not satisfactory, because they were so heavy that they could not be drawn by one horse. An American born local coachbuilder who had his premises off City Road was then instructed to produce a further eight cars of more conventional design, which would be lighter and thus would need only one horse. They duly appeared, but the builder had omitted to use conventional girder stays, which resulted in the platforms becoming detached from the bodies.

In 1885/6 the new manager, John Gardner, had every car rebuilt save an additional one which had been constructed by the well-known firm of GF Milnes & Co in Birkenhead and also bought two more, built by Starbuck. Gardner then purchased a twelfth car which had garden, as opposed to knifeboard, seats, on top and some of the others were then rebuilt to that pattern. Gardner was born in Scotland in 1850 but was to have a long association with Chester.

In 1886 the company hired car 9 to an engineering firm, Hughes & Lancaster, who converted it as an experimental compressed air powered tramcar. That company then seem to have purchased the car from the operating company, and they then converted it to a single-decker, in order to reduce weight. Despite considerable efforts and modifications, however, a persistent problem involving the sudden loss of pressure was never completely overcome. It is not clear whether the car ever ran regularly in passenger service, whether as a double- or single-decker.

Apart from this unsatisfactory experiment, the company ran its service satisfactorily. It was assisted financially by the abolition of the toll charges on the Grosvenor Bridge in 1885; a yearly payment in lieu of conventional fees had been paid before that. There was a vast increase in traffic every May, when the race meeting was held, and this strained the resources, as thousands arrived at the station needing transport to the course. It seems probable that during that time a second or trace horse was used to assist with the laden cars: otherwise, spare horses were kept only at Saltney, where there was an incline up to the terminus, and sometimes to assist over the canal bridge in City Road, and they were used when required.

The company also began running its own horse bus services, initially one from the Bache (Liverpool Road) to Christleton Road (Cherry Orchard) and the other from the Market Square to Hoole Church. Summer excursions were also run to the Grosvenor family seat at Eaton Hall, and to WE Gladstone's home at Hawarden.

The success of the company undertaking and the growth of municipal operation across the country encouraged Chester to exercise its statutory powers under the Tramways Act 1870. These enabled the local authority to serve notice to purchase within six months of the 21st anniversary of the passing of the 1878 Act, a period which began on 22 July 1899. This was done, and on 9 August 1901 the Chester Corporation Act gave the council power to construct and run tramways and to use electric power on them. The company system was taken over with effect from 1 January 1902, at a cost to the purchasers of £19,866. Mr Gardner transferred his employment to the Council, as did most of the other employees.

The Council continued to run the horse-powered trams until it had carried out the required works, but passenger numbers increased immediately because a decision was made to allow graduated fares rather than the flat fares used previously, which made a trip from the city centre to the General Station proportionately expensive.

The Act provided not only for electrification, but also for the reduction of the gauge to 3 feet 6 inches. The objective was to double most of the track and thus eliminate the delays caused by the passing loops, which were in any event less practicable because of the increase in traffic. The only exception was the narrow Eastgate Street, where passing loops were retained.

It was also provided that the Saltney line should be extended by less than 100 yards, so that it almost reached the railway bridge, but remained wholly in England; the bridge was too low to permit trams to run underneath it. Two new lines were authorised to the east of the city. These were both relatively short and each stopped just short of the city boundary. The first was to continue along Boughton from the point where the trams to the station turned north and then to proceed along Tarvin Road to finish near the junction with Filkins Lane. The Boughton section was to be double-tracked but that on Tarvin Road was to be single-tracked with two passing places. The second extension was to leave the first at the junction of Boughton and Tarvin Road and continued along Christleton Road to Stocks Lane; again the last section was single-track, but with only one passing place. Authority was also given to extend the Christleton Road line along Chapel Lane and Filkins Lane, so that it would meet the Tarvin Road line, but that was never built and indeed no bus service was ever thereafter run along the two narrow lanes.

There were originally proposals for other lines towards the north of the city but these were dropped during the Parliamentary procedure.

There was some opposition to the use of overhead wires in the historic centre of the city, but fortunately the surface-contact system, which brought about problems wherever it was used, was not adopted.

The conversion required the expenditure of considerable funds. The initial step was the reconstruction of the original line, for which an estimate of just over £40,000 was accepted. Then 12 cars were ordered from Milnes, who by that date had moved to Wellington, Shropshire. The cost of these was £575 each. The total initial cost of this work, including the cost of purchase of the horse tram undertaking itself, was at modern values about £7 million. The problem with small systems such as Chester was the burden of debt was very high, and passenger numbers were insufficient to permit the expenditure of further sums on modernisation.

The trams themselves were relatively small and had open tops, which they retained throughout. They were of conventional design, save that in place of the more usual panelling with hessian lining they had unlined sheet steel panels, which made them very much noisier than most cars of that era. The livery was apple green and ivory with lining out.

After the work had been completed, which had necessitated a break in the service, the electric trams began service on 6 April 1903. The existing depot in City Road was reconstructed, which included raising the roof to accept the trolley poles and the wires. Pits were also constructed, and the former stables were rebuilt in order to become a repair shop and for storage. Two short streets giving access to the depot were named Tramway Street and Car Street.

The new cars were a huge improvement on that which had been provided before and were much appreciated. However, the residents of east Chester were anxious that the authorised extensions should be constructed as soon as possible: this was not the subject of any urgent action by the Council, but in early 1906 contracts were signed and on 22 November of that year services were commenced. The cost was in excess of £12,000, or at modern values about another £1.5 million. Cars on the new routes terminated in the centre and there was no through running from them to Saltney.

In 1906 a 20-seat one man or "demi" car arrived, but it did not prove successful because of the limited capacity and was relegated to snowplough and other ancillary duties. However, during 1907 a further five conventional cars arrived. Milnes had gone out of business by this time, and they were built by the United Electric Car Company of Preston. On 9 September 1912 it was reported that four tramway motors had been offered to the Council by the Metropolitan Electric Tramways, but it was resolved not to proceed further with the offer.

No further extensions were constructed, although in 1914 Chester RDC planned to have the Tarvin Road service extended about half a mile into its area, purchased some rail and prepared a Bill for authority to do so, but the outbreak of the war put paid to the idea and it was never resurrected.

When consideration was being given to the takeover of the horse tramways, the Council also gave consideration to purchasing the horse buses which were also run by the Chester Tramways Company. This was first discussed in November 1901, at which time the services being run were from the Market Square north to the Bache, and also east to Tarvin Road, Christleton Road and Hoole. It was decided not to purchase that part of the undertaking, but under the Act of 1901 the Council was, of course, given the power to construct electric tramways along Tarvin and Christleton Roads. Further, the Chester Corporation Act 1901, by section 53, gave the Council the power to run buses powered either by horse or by mechanical power in connection with or in prolongation of the tramways and in particular from Bridge Street to Eccleston Lodge, from the Station to the Roodee (the racecourse), from Canal Street to Saughall Road (Stone Bridge), and from the Town Hall Square to both Upton and Hoole Village. None of these powers were exercised and the mention of mechanical power at that early stage was very unusual.

The issue of buses next arose in 1905, and resulted from the perceived reluctance of the Council to extend the system to the Boughton area and beyond. A letter was received asking for buses to be used in lieu of trams, but, at a public meeting, local residents urged that instead progress be made with the tramway, and that was then done. However, the fact that buses were being mooted led to requests from residents of both Liverpool Road and the Bache, in the north of the city, and Handbridge, in the south. In June 1905 the Council took the decision to proceed with the tramway extension but agreed to defer for 12 months the question of using buses. Deferring issues was a frequent solution adopted by local authorities to avoid having to take a decision, but it is fair to say that it was still a very early date to think about running motor buses.

When the matter was reconsidered in 1906 further requests were made by those living in Liverpool Road and the Council gave consideration to the commencement of a number of services, including to Cheyney Road and to Appleyards Lane (Handbridge). It was eventually recommended by the Tramways Committee that three buses should be purchased and should be used to provide a service every 15 minutes to the Bache and another to Cheyney Road (Canal Bridge). This was sometimes referred to as Saughall Road, into which Cheyney Road ran.

The trams carried fleet numbers on their dashes but the photographic emulsion of the day failed to 'see' the colours correctly. This is car No 2.

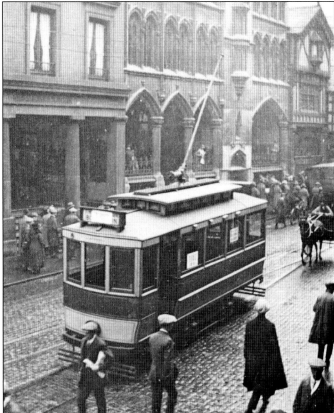

The demi-car was pressed into service on Race Days, as here and is seen in East Street. *(Both MTMS)*

This decision was then the subject of a Special Meeting of the City Council on 10 April 1907. The full Council decided by 13 votes to 11 not to endorse the views of the Tramways Committee. An opportunity was undoubtedly lost, which if taken would have enabled the local authority to begin services into the areas where Crosville was to run. Crosville had been set up by members of the Crosland Taylor family, led by Claude, in 1906, and in 1911 they moved into the provision of bus services, the first route being from Chester to Ellesmere Port. Thereafter, from their headquarters at Crane Wharf in the city, they expanded rapidly and the new services included local routes in north and east Chester.

1907 was, however, still a very early date for the Council to decide on the running of a reliable service with motor vehicles.

Instead of running their own service, Council representatives then spoke to Henry H Aldred, who was by then running a horse bus to and from the Bache. Aldred was a man of many parts, as he was also a veterinary surgeon; in later life he abandoned transport and combined his treatment of animals with farming. The Council suggested to Aldred that he trial a service to the Cheyney Road area, which he did for a short time, but it did not prove successful.

The issue of transport to the Liverpool Road area would not go away. A further request was made in October 1912, and the correspondent was told that in the near future the committee would consider the whole question of providing buses for those districts which were not already served and that the town clerk, the electrical engineer and the tramways manager would be asked to obtain information about running buses and the cost of doing so.

On 28 November 1912 the tramways committee was given information about correspondence with Daimler, who offered to send a demonstrator. It was suggested that a service be started from the Bache across the city to Handbridge; however, Gardner was not enthusiastic and thought there would be a loss on such a service, and a greater loss if it were run by double-deckers.

In December 1912 Daimler duly sent a demonstrator for the Tramways Committee to examine, but yet again no decision to proceed was taken. The 40 horse-power bus ran from Chester via Liverpool Road, Welsh Road, the Queensferry Bridge, Hawarden and Saltney back to the city. Nothing happened in consequence of this.

In about early 1915 Aldred discontinued all his services, and on 13 January 1915 a further letter of request for buses was sent to the Council. Claude Crosland Taylor had attended a meeting of those concerned locally and at that he offered to hire a bus to the Council at the rate of 9½d a mile. The Council appeared to be interested in running a service to Upton, and Eaton Road (Handbridge) was also considered. The electrical engineer was instructed to prepare a scheme for providing a motor bus service.

He reported back that the charge proposed by Crosville was reasonable and that using only one bus services could be run from the Town Hall to Saughall Road (Canal Bridge) and to Upton (Wheatsheaf); Handbridge appeared to have been forgotten. The scheme went as far as timetables being prepared, giving approximately an hourly service on each leg, and then a further schedule was drawn up for services to Saughall Road and to the Bache. The engineer suggested that electric buses be used, by which he meant trolleybuses, and that they should be one-man operated. It was, however, then decided that no progress should be made until the end of the war.

On 8 July 1915 Hoole UDC wrote to Chester saying that Crosville were proposing a service to Newton-by-Chester and asking the City Council if they would be prepared to commit themselves to £250, which was half the guarantee asked for by the company. The answer was no.

Mr Gardner had remained in post throughout this period, which gave continuity to the undertaking, but he died in September 1915, by which time he was in any event almost at retirement age. The Council seemed reluctant to commit themselves to a replacement and resolved to advertise only for a traffic superintendent. This was William H Ellis, who was born in Chester in 1882 and whose working life was spent in the service of the undertaking. It was 3 January 1918 before he was finally designated as General Manager, a position he was to hold until 1943. His salary was increased from £120 to £150 per annum, but was increased considerably after the war. He had previously been a teacher of electrical engineering at the Grosvenor Museum in the city.

In August 1917 Stewart Bill, the permanent way engineer of Birmingham Corporation,

A lively scene in Bridge Street, the motor traffic now commonplace.

Eastgate Street, with its famous clock and passing loop for the trams. *(Both MTMS)*

inspected the track and said that it "could not be said to be in good condition", which was perhaps a classic British understatement.

The lack of maintenance which had been undertaken during the hostilities accentuated the poor state of the track and of the cars. On 7 October 1920 it was resolved that four tram trucks be purchased and the Corporation would then build bodies on them; whether it was projected that they should have top covers fitted is not recorded. In any event, this never happened.

On 13 December 1920 the tramways sub-committee reported that a large amount needed to be spent on the cars and that more maintenance was required, particularly on the wheels, and that consideration should be given to replacing the entire system either with trolleybuses or motor buses. In January 1921 Ellis himself reported that only the five newest cars, dating from 1907, were fit for much longer service but that even they required the replacement of most of their electrical equipment, and that all the Milnes cars should be replaced immediately as they were at the end of their economic life. The little-used demi-car was said to be in better condition than any of the others.

In January 1921 it was resolved to invite tenders for 20 new buses, and in February 1921 a number of quotes were received, from several firms for motor buses and from Clough Smith for trolleybuses. Then on 14 March 1921 the tramways sub-committee said that the track should be taken up from the Castle to Saltney and be replaced by buses. That was an absurd proposition, as it would have meant that passengers from Saltney could not be carried right into town, never mind to the General Station. It is also interesting that Claude Crosland Taylor, the founder of Crosville, which was expanding rapidly at this time, was not only on the Council but was on the tramways sub-committee. There was an obvious conflict of interest.

On 18 April 1921 it was resolved that AR Fearnley, the General Manager of the substantial Sheffield undertaking, should be invited to report on the state of the tramways and on the various options available. Shortly after that decision had been taken, Liverpool contacted Chester to say that they had 20 surplus buses available to sell, but, of course, no action could be taken on that.

On 15 November 1921 Arthur Fearnley submitted his report. He made the underlying point of importance, which was that £82,380 had been expended on capital expenditure for the system, and that at that date £57,714 was still outstanding. He said that there was still 7 to 8 years of life in the permanent way from the Castle to Saltney, and that there was no need to replace it at that time. In particular, he said that it was not in any event sensible to have buses only on that section. He was strongly against allowing services in the area to be run by an outside company and said there was no reason why new bus services could not be started.

The Council accepted what Fearnley said and that enabled them not to grasp the nettle. On 2 March 1922 the city surveyor said he did not agree with the conclusions of the report, but on 22 March 1922 the Council decided that the tramways should continue for the next seven or eight years, by which time they would be really worn out, but that £12,000 should be expended on the track and overhead. The issue of running buses was ignored in reaching these conclusions.

All the cars still had open tops and when that was raised again, the Ministry of Transport in a letter dated 5 September 1923 vetoed the introduction of roofs because of the perceived danger of overturning if narrow gauge trams were too top heavy, a risk that was thought to be particularly applicable to the open Grosvenor Bridge section.

It seems clear that by this time it was being generally accepted that the tramway had a limited life, but no long-term plan was being drawn up by the local authority.

In November 1924 Ellis raised the issue of buses again, because Chester was to host the Royal Agricultural Show. It was proposed that a service be run from the General Station to the Showground; however, it was then decided that Crosville should be permitted to run it, on the basis that they paid an amount per passenger to the Council. On 19 February 1925 Crosville agreed to run the service on the basis that they remitted 25% of the receipts to Chester.

Shortly after this, on 11 March 1925 the Council inspected a Shelvoke & Drewry Freighter bus, but it is not clear how that came about. However, following the demonstration, Ellis was asked on 2 April 1925 to prepare a report for the Council on the provision of a municipal service using motor buses or "trackless trams" as trolleybuses were then termed. His report was ready by 2 July 1925, but the committee deferred consideration of it until September, then again to October.

On 8 October 1925 the matter was finally debated and the committee resolved to attempt running motor bus services and that the Manager should hire (not purchase) three for that purpose. They were relying on the powers given under the Act of 1901 to run bus services ancillary to the tramways.

It was then recommended that the Council should hire, rather than buy, three Guy 26-seat single-deckers, in order to operate a cross-city service from Hoole Road, in the north-east, at the junction with Hare Lane, down Hoole Road, Brook Street and Frodsham Street, then St John Street, Pepper Street, Lower Bridge Street and Handbridge, to terminate in Eaton Road, in the south, at the junction with Percy Road; neither leg would have supported a tram or trolleybus service. It was suggested that the hire be for six months, to test the viability of the service.

On 27 January 1926 the full Council considered the matter and referred it back to the tramways committee for further reports on cost. It is notable that Claude Crosland Taylor did not vote on this, appreciating his adverse interest. More estimates were given and it was resolved that the buses should be two-man operated, which of course affected the economics of the proposed operation adversely.

Having got this far, there were objections by Hoole UDC, through the territory of which most of the northern leg would have run, and by some local unions. On 24 February 1926 it was decided by the Council that the recommendations of the committee should not be approved but rather that there should be a review of the whole tramway system and the policy for passenger transport in Chester should be defined.

It is notable however that it appears that a Bill was put forward in parliament to permit bus operation but it was refused a Second Reading.

The question of defining policy came before the new Tramways (Motor Omnibus Services) Sub-Committee on 11 June 1926 and predictably was adjourned.

The next development was that in 1927 Crosville approached the Council proposing that they acquire the undertaking and replace the trams with their own buses. The local authority

on the other hand remained anxious that they should retain control of local transport and refuted Crosville. When WJ Crosland Taylor wrote the first part of his history of the company, *The Sowing and the Harvest*, in 1948, he reflected that Chester City Council was at that period "rightly jealous of its rights and privileges" which led to a period of difficulties between the two. Chester was indeed somewhat defensive, not least because of the financial state of its operation.

In March 1928 the Tramways Committee of the Council was given a comprehensive report which set out the various possible ways forward, including modernisation of the trams, replacing them with trolleybuses, replacing them with motor buses, or selling the undertaking to an outside company (in other words to Crosville). They recommended that the Council should continue to run the service, but made it clear that since £72,697 was required to modernise the trams that was an impossible route to take. They were against partial replacement for the same reasons as had been put forward earlier and concluded that petrol-engined motor buses were the preferred way forward and that 13 double-deckers seating 50 or 52 were required.

This led to a period of political controversy. The Committee recommended that application be made for a Parliamentary Bill giving the Council power to abandon the tramways and to give them the authority to operate petrol-engined motor buses anywhere within a five-mile radius of the Cross. Because the city boundary was so tightly drawn, that provision would have enabled Chester to operate out of its area and to serve some of the growing villages. It would also have enabled it to run on the local services in the north east of the city on which Crosville had established themselves, many of which were then partly in the Urban District of Hoole, which reached almost to the back of the General Station. James Crosland Taylor, in his history already mentioned, misrecollected this proposal and said that Chester wanted a ten-mile radius, which would have enabled them to reach Ellesmere Port, which is nine miles from Chester. However, the contemporary records are quite clear that the proposal was for five miles.

The Council were advised (correctly) that they needed a new Act, because the powers given by the 1901 Act applied only to running buses ancillary to the trams and not to replacing them completely.

The matter was of such consequence that it was referred to the full Council, where a very lengthy and extremely acrimonious debate ensued on 28 March 1928. It was proposed at one point that the issue be re-remitted to the Tramways Committee, a classic local authority manoeuvre to avoid having to take a decision. However, this was not done and in due course the recommendations of the Committee were accepted by a single vote, including the suggestion that the power should extend to five miles around the Cross.

Crosville were extremely perturbed by the prospect of Chester increasing its sphere of operation, as were Western Transport of Wrexham (later absorbed by Crosville), which ran south from Chester into Wales.

It seems unlikely in any event that, in the pre-Road Traffic Act era, Parliamentary authority would have been granted for powers over the large area which Chester sought. The peculiarity of the situation here was that Crosville were already operating local services within the area of the authority - a situation which occurred also in Brighton and in Southend and led eventually in both of those places to the running of joint services in a designated area.

The dispute over the replacement of trams in Chester also has to be seen against the background of changes which were occurring in the Crosville business. The Railways (Road Transport) Acts 1928 gave the railway companies clear powers to involve themselves in bus operation, whereas previously these had been subject to some dispute. The policy was then adopted by the railway companies of buying into existing bus companies rather than starting completely new enterprises. The LMS saw Crosville as a prime target for investment and the family-owned company was short of capital and wanted to expand further, especially in North Wales, where at this time it had not secured the lucrative traffic on the coast.

The LMS approached Crosville early in 1929. In August 1929 an acceptable offer was made and in November of that year Crosville went into voluntary liquidation. As part of the agreement, Claude and James Crosland Taylor remained as managers of the business, but they now had capital resources to back them up.

In 1930 a national agreement was made between the four large railway companies and the Tilling and British Automobile Traction Group that the railways would acquire 50% of the share capital in most of the companies under the control of the latter, but conversely would divest themselves of 50% of those shareholdings in companies which they wholly controlled, one of which was Crosville. Thus, after about 9 months of being run as a wholly-owned subsidiary of the LMS Railway, from 15 May 1930 a new Crosville company was set up on the basis of being owned 50% by the railway and 50% by Tillings.

It was as all these matters were occurring that it was necessary for Crosville to deal with what was perceived as the threat from Chester. In 1928 Crosville were attempting to establish a service to Vicar's Cross; the Council decided to oppose that before their own Watch Committee, which reveals clearly how the system worked at that time.

On 23 January 1929 a meeting was held between the local authority and the various bus companies, headed by Claude Crosland Taylor. It was suggested by Taylor and his colleagues that the radius should be reduced to three miles. However, general agreement was reached that it should instead be 3½ miles, that Chester would not compete over existing company services, and that the companies would not pick up and set down on Chester's routes. It was also agreed that with cooperation with others, services could run for up to 11 miles from the Cross but this part of the Act turned out to be a dead letter.

On one level, this represented a victory for Crosville, which preserved its routes within the city limits and in Hoole, which became much more lucrative when the area in question was developed after the Second World War, but it also enabled the Corporation to move forward knowing where they could start new services without powerful opposition. Chester thus paid the price for not starting bus services earlier, when the opportunity was available.

The concord enabled the council to place before Parliament an Act to allow them to abandon the tramway and to run buses, and that Act was unopposed by the other interests. This became the Chester Corporation Act 1929 and it received Royal assent on 10 May of that year. Once it was passed the Council shook off its previous dilatory approach and proceeded with considerable expedition.

On 12 June 1929 James Dalrymple, the General Manager of the very substantial Glasgow municipal operation, was asked to advise on the commencement of bus services; the detail is set out in Chapter 4.

Bus operation eventually began on 12 February 1930 and the last trams ran in the afternoon of 15 February. The very next day, contractors began removing the cars and dismantling them. Although some parts went to Liverpool for spares, none of the trams was sold for further service. In that respect, Chester was typical of systems of its size; they cost so much to construct that modernisation and extension was not possible, and in any event the city remained at this time small and traffic to many outer areas was limited.

Race day again, showing congestion caused as an abnormal number of cars wait to use the passing loop. *(MTMS)*

4: BUS OPERATION 1930-39

Chester had, as we have seen, had a number of opportunities to start bus operation before it decided to replace the trams, but took none of them. Ultimately, that was to its disadvantage, in that it was effectively put in a position where it had to accommodate the company operators, especially Crosville, which had been permitted to start running within its boundaries and in the adjoining areas. The period of paralysis caused by the decision not to accede in 1922 to the General Manager's recommendation to replace the trams then gave a significant advantage to Crosville, which expanded rapidly in the immediate post-1918 years.

By the time that the decision was finally taken to replace the trams, Chester had also to think about extra services with its new buses, and to consider dealing with the many issues of expansion it had shelved over the years.

On 21 June 1929 it was resolved that the Council should run its initial bus services as follows:

- Town Hall to Saltney;
- Town Hall to Vicar's Cross, Littleton,
- Christleton and back to the Town Hall, in both directions;
- General Station to Town Hall and Saughall Road (Stone Bridge).

It was always intended that the Saltney route should be extended into the Welsh part of the settlement, to a point also known, confusingly, as Stone Bridge, but later as West View. West View was a private road, which has now disappeared, into or from which it was intended that vehicles would reverse off the main road, but Hawarden RDC raised objections to that and the extension had to be deferred. Any service to Christleton village would be restricted to single-deckers because of the canal bridge on the approach, which would not bear the weight of double-deckers. However, the proposed circular was soon abandoned, as the Council were told that in any event Littleton Lane, between Vicar's Cross and Christleton, was too narrow at that time for a bus service.

In January 1930 AEC Regent II, with Short Bros of Rochester body, was the first vehicle to arrive in Chester to begin the replacement of the trams. *(OS)*

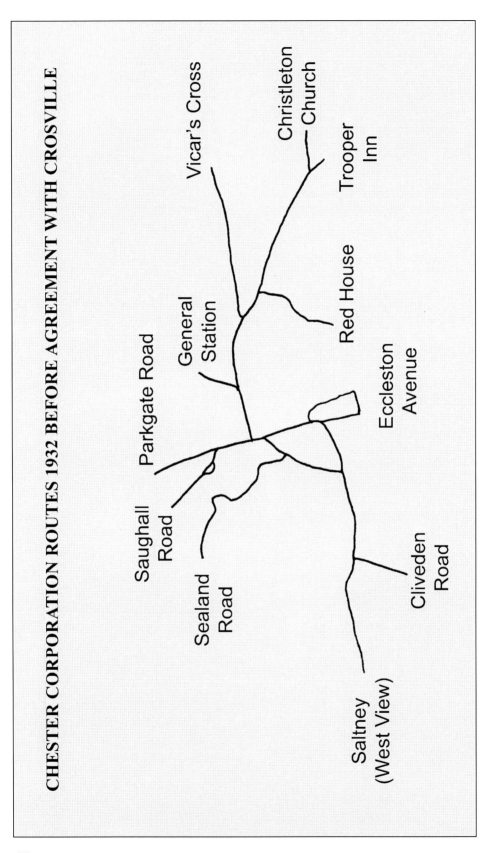

On 30 August 1929 Chester agreed to accept a tender by AEC for 16 single-deckers. Perhaps perversely on 19 September 1929 no fewer than six firms submitted double-deckers for inspection. It was then decided to rescind the previous decision and instead purchase ten single- and six double-deckers.

On 28 November 1929 it was resolved that in the future the municipal operation should be termed the Transport Undertaking, and the manager should be known as the General Manager.

In order to effect the tramway conversion, Chester thus purchased 16 new AECs, all bodied by Shorts. Ten of these were Regal single-deckers with 30-seat dual-door bodies; there were six Regent double-deckers with seating for 50. They arrived ready for the commencement of the new services. All were petrol-engined, as would be expected at that time.

On 26 March 1930, just after services had started running, the City Council ordered a further four Regents, which arrived in June.

These buses were logically numbered 1 to 10 (single-deckers) and 11 to 20 (double-deckers) and all but the last four were given consecutive registration numbers, but for some reason they were not given fleet numbers in corresponding order. All the double-deckers which arrived then or later were of conventional highbridge layout. Chester had no bridges which required the use of lowbridge vehicles, not even the famous bridge with clock across Eastgate Street. The tram depot was modified so that it could hold 22 buses.

The services were not initially numbered. As introduced, they were as follows:

- General Station to Saughall Road (Canal Bridge) via the Cross and Garden Lane;
- Saltney (Wood Street) to Vicar's Cross (Old Toll Bar) via Grosvenor Bridge, the Cross and Tarvin Road;
- Saltney (Wood Street) to Christleton Church via Grosvenor Bridge, the Cross and Christleton Road.

In this way, new ground was broken with the long-awaited Saughall Road section, and the services from Saltney were linked with the Boughton area rather than with the General Station. Both the former tram services were extended eastwards and both now went a considerable distance beyond the city boundary. The Saltney services originally ended at the tram terminus, just on the Chester side of the railway bridge.

One of the original AEC Regals with Short's dual-entrance bodies, 7, lies over at the town hall terminus. Readers may be confused by the apparent differences in livery in these photographs. The buses continued to carry the light green colour the trams had carried, but as previously noted, the film of the day could render this darker, as here, or lighter, as in the next view. *(OS)*

The tramlines are still visible as Regent 12 proceeds through the city centre bound for Saltney. *(OS)*

These initial arrangements did not last long. As early as 17 March 1930 an unspecified alteration was made to the Saughall Road service: it appears that when introduced it ran out via Canal Street and Raymond Street, in via Garden Lane and then further along Garden Lane to terminate across the canal bridge itself, probably near the junction with Salisbury Street. It is not clear what minor change was made at this time.

Then, in May 1930, the buses from Vicar's Cross were extended into Saltney Town, and thus into Wales, and a turning point was constructed at the junction with West View. This was well beyond the previous terminus and so served the village of Saltney rather than only its outskirts. It met with the objections of the Welsh local authority and involved tortuous negotiations in order to acquire the land required for a terminus.

At the same time, the Christleton service was also altered. Only alternate buses thereafter served Christleton Church; the others ran to the Trooper Inn, which was on the outskirts of the village and involved a short further run along the main Whitchurch Road rather than going into the centre of the settlement. It was thus possible to run double-deckers on that leg; the forecourt of the pub was used to reverse, which required reversing off the main road, which was to lead to trouble much later.

All the Christleton services were also taken off the Grosvenor Bridge and ran instead via the Dee Bridge and Handbridge, where there was much more local traffic available. Finally, there was a very short extension at Saltney beyond Wood Street to the Anchor Hotel, which was on the boundary between England and Wales and, appropriately, on the corner of Boundary Lane; this applied only to the two Christleton services, as the Vicar's Cross buses had already been extended into Wales.

As these new services were being inaugurated, there was a further approach from Crosville, newly resolute after its takeover the previous year by the LMS. On 3 June 1930 there was a meeting in London, attended by representatives from Chester, Crosville, Tillings (BAT), the LMS and the GWR. It was again suggested that the corporation undertaking as a whole be purchased; this was again rejected by the local authority. The Council did however say that they would consider a coordination scheme.

Proposed terms for this were set out in a letter dated 13 October 1930; it was written by Claude Crosland Taylor, as one of the provisions of the agreement between Crosville and the railway had been that the family should continue to run the buses. Claude Crosland Taylor's conflict of interest was nowhere more apparent that at this time, as he was still a City Councillor and indeed had been Mayor of Chester in 1926/7.

No agreement was reached at this stage because the Council had decided to attempt to extend its boundaries and, in fact, after a long delay, lodged a Bill to that effect in December 1931. The aim was to absorb the Urban District of Hoole into Chester, an entirely logical step. On 1 December 1930 the City Council's Coordination of Services Sub-Committee resolved not to consider Crosland Taylor's proposals until after the resolution of the proposals to extend the city.

Many members of local authorities took the view that they were entitled to run services within their own boundaries, regardless of who had been providing services before. That may have been the position when the authority itself was licensing local operations (and thus in many cases acting as applicant and judge in the same cause) but it was certainly not the case under the Road Traffic Act 1930, which of course was contemporaneous with these discussions, and came fully into force with effect from 9 February 1931.

The main effect of the new Act so far as licensing was concerned was that all decisions were taken by the Traffic Commissioners, who were independent of any of the parties: however, in practice the years ahead were to show that existing operators were protected and that the interests of the travelling public were not regarded as of prime importance.

There was another crucial series of provisions in what was intended originally as a freestanding Act, but which then became Part V of the 1930 Act. That provided that by section 101 if a local authority had powers to operate a tram, trolleybus or bus undertaking within its own boundaries, it did not need further statutory powers to operate anywhere within them or indeed outside of them, but it did in the latter case need the consent of the Commissioners not only to run the service but to run outside of its own area. The argument about the radius within which Chester could operate under its 1929 Act thus became irrelevant.

Chester, which had been so sluggish in its reaction to calls for more services, was apparently reinvigorated by having finally taken the decision to scrap the trams.

After the alterations to the first services, a completely new route was opened up on 6 June 1930. This ran from the General Station into the town centre and then along Grosvenor Street to

A posed view of 12, labelled for the special service to the Races. *(OS)*

The tramlines are also still visible in the view of AEC Regent 14, passing under the Eastgate Street bridge en route for the General Station. Note the distinctive shape of the Short Bros roof. *(OS)*

the Castle. It then turned a sharp right via Nicholas Street into Watergate Street and then Crane Street, passed around the Dee Basin, incidentally serving the Crosville headquarters at Crane Wharf; it terminated in Sealand Road, near the then Chester FC stadium; the club was to join the Football League in 1931. The area around was otherwise however not much developed. The Council initially wanted to run straight from the Cross into Watergate Street, avoiding the Castle, but was refused permission for this. On 26 November 1930 Chester was asked to run a circular service around Sealand Road but the General Manager said that what was being offered could not be improved upon.

Not content with this, two further services which were begun before 1930 came to an end. On 17 October a General Station-Parkgate Road route began, again via the Cross. The Parkgate Road section was quite short and ended just before the Cheshire Lines railway bridge. It is interesting that no attempt was made at this time to run along the Liverpool Road, which had been the subject of so much debate and was near Parkgate Road. However, by this time Crosville was well established on that line, which formed part of by far the most remunerative service on its entire vast network, the Birkenhead-Chester direct route.

The last service introduced that year began on 19 December. It was a cross-city service from Handbridge (Eccleston Avenue), where there was a large terminal loop, with buses running out via Eaton Road and returning via Eccleston Avenue itself and Hartington Street, then through the centre and to the east, turning off Christleton Road down Stocks Lane and on to Dee Banks, where it finished at the Red House, on the corner with Keristal Avenue, just outside the city boundary and, as its name implied, by the river. Chester RDC wanted the service to run via Heath Lane and Becketts Lane instead of Stocks Lane, but Chester City said that Becketts Lane was not suitable for buses.

As well as these developments, it was resolved on 5 June 1930 that Littleton Lane be improved and that the canal bridge leading to Christleton should be rebuilt, which would have enabled the planned circular to be run. This canal bridge became another long-running saga. On 4 September 1930 the Council agreed to contribute £500 towards the work required to Littleton Lane but in 1931 it declined to pay anything at all towards the work needed at Christleton.

Chester was able to run all these new services without purchasing further vehicles. It did however hire six double-deckers with crews from

Birkenhead for the three race days in May, which always strained the fleet, and it continued to do that subsequently.

On 5 March 1931 both Chester and Crosville were asked to contribute towards the strengthening of the Saughall Road canal bridge, over which they were both running. They both refused and Chester said they would discontinue their service over it. A group of local residents complained and suggested that the service be terminated at the junction of Cheyney Road and Garden Lane, so on the town side rather than the far side of the bridge. The resolution of this is not clear, but the service over the bridge was not abandoned.

Chester's newly expansive mood continued into 1931. On 30 April 1931 it was decided to apply to the Traffic Commissioners to run a circular from the Town Hall via Brook Street, Ermine Road, Brook Lane and Liverpool Road back to the starting point. Although this did attempt, at last, to run along Liverpool Road, it was only aimed at the inner portion and did not reach the Bache area, which had been the subject of so much debate. It also ran through Hoole, and Chester may have taken the view that since that area was to be incorporated into the city in the near future there would then not be subject to the need for a separate application under S101 for permission to run out of the area. However, the plan for extension of the city was proceeding slowly.

This was the first application which was brought under the new Act. However, it was opposed not only by Crosville (predictably) but also by Hoole and by Cheshire County Council. The preliminary application by Chester for permission to run outside its area was heard on 15 September 1931 at Chester Town Hall.

At that hearing, Chester was granted licences for its existing routes, subject to coordinating its provisions with Crosville and to full protection being given to its old tram routes, but permission was refused to run out of area into Hoole. The final nail in this coffin was that on 4 January 1932 a poll of ratepayers rejected the idea of extension of the city, the Bill for which was then withdrawn.

In 1936 the issue of enlargement of the city returned, but this time there was no question of absorbing Hoole. What happened then was that the former civil parish of Newton was divided between Chester CBC and Hoole UDC, with the

One of Crosville's Lions passing some intrepid window cleaners – no health and safety here. Crosville's buses were about to change to maroon livery following the purchase of the company by the LMS railway. *(STA)*

latter taking about two thirds of the area and with other adjustments roughly doubling its size. It was at this time also that Blacon cum Crabwall was absorbed into the city.

Hoole was not finally incorporated into Chester until 1 April 1954, by which time the pattern of bus services was very well established. However, all but a very small portion of Upton by Chester remained for the time outside the city, as indeed did Great Boughton and the Welsh part of Saltney.

1931, in fact, turned out to be a much quieter year than 1930. On 13 July 1931 it was agreed that a further four Regents be purchased, but after the refusal of permission for the Hoole circular this was amended to two. It was December 1931 when these further Regents arrived, this time with Weymann 50-seat bodies.

It has already been shown that Chester was willing to ask outsiders to advise them. On 13 October 1931 the coordination sub-committee asked whether John Barnard, the General Manager of the Bolton undertaking, would advise them on the issues being raised by Crosville; he agreed to do so. In the same period the Council wrote to the Commissioners saying that an application before them by Crosville to run to Piper's Ash and Guilden Sutton be considered without prejudice to plans for coordination.

In January 1932 the service from Christleton (Trooper Inn) was extended to West View in Saltney, but the Christleton Village service continued to turn at the Anchor Hotel.

A timetable has survived in the Bus Archive which can be dated to the period between January and June 1932. It was quite a simple narrow sheet, but it was comprehensible as the services were then so straightforward.

At that time, the services being operated, with the normal weekday frequencies were thus:

- General Station-Cross-Town Hall-Saughall Road (Canal Bridge), every 15 minutes;
- General Station-Cross-Sealand Road, every 30 minutes;
- General Station-Cross-Town Hall-Parkgate Road, every 30 minutes (running through from Eccleston Avenue on Sundays only);
- Eccleston Avenue-Cross-Red House, every 40 minutes;
- Saltney (Anchor)-Cross-Christleton Church, every 24 minutes;
- Saltney (West View and Anchor)-Cross-Christleton (Trooper Inn), every 12 minutes;
- Saltney (West View and Anchor)-Cross-Vicar's Cross, every 12 minutes.

On 7 January 1932 Barnard submitted a positive report on the proposed agreement with Crosville and it was agreed that it should be approved. It was finally signed on 24 June 1932 and came into effect on 1 July 1932.

In the meantime, on 20 June 1932 a new service was commenced from the General Station to Eccleston Avenue, which did not involve the use of any new routings. On the same day another new service began, which expanded the mileage somewhat. It too ran from the General Station via the Cross and Handbridge and followed the Saltney buses along Hough Green, but turned south into Cliveden Road to serve a new housing estate, which was to become an important source of traffic over the years. The area was properly called Lache, but destination blinds showed Cliveden Road.

The 1932 agreement was seminal to the way in which Chester ran its services thereafter and was treated by all concerned with considerable reverence.

There were some considerable advantages to Chester in the agreement. Crosville agreed that it would not pick up passengers coming into town or drop them off in the other direction, for 440 yards beyond Great Saughall, Vicar's Cross, Christleton Village, the Trooper Inn, Red House on Dee Banks and Saltney (West View). It also agreed not to object to the Council's services to Piper's Ash, Vicar's Cross or Christleton.

Chester, on the other hand, agreed not to operate within the sector between and including Liverpool Road round to Hoole Road and Warrington Road, a considerable reciprocal concession. Because of the failure of the proposal to extend the city, much of that area was in any event then within Hoole rather than in Chester and only a small part of the area concerned was within the city boundary.

There was also an important exchange of operations: Chester agreed to discontinue its services to Sealand Road and to Parkgate Road and to allow Crosville to operate on them. Some considerable time later, Chester did begin running up Parkgate Road again, in order to achieve access to the eastern side of the new Blacon estate, but neither that nor the canal bridge giving access to the area had been constructed in 1932. For many years Crosville continued to operate along Sealand Road, extending the service to Blacon Point, but the area never became much built up and its frequency was not better than hourly.

Chester in its turn took over two Crosville services. The first was in the event to be the basis of the most intensive services in the city, but that was not apparent at that time. It ran over the Cheyney Road canal bridge, along Saughall Road, through Blacon and then the hamlet of Little Saughall, and terminated at the Greyhound Inn in the village of Great Saughall, well outside the city boundary. This service did not use Garden Lane, but turned left into Chichester Street at the point where the Liverpool and Parkgate Roads converged, then turned right into Bouverie Street and then left into Cheyney Road, where it met the Saughall Road service. It too ran near, but not across, the border with Wales, as a considerable area on the north side of the River Dee is in that country, and is known as Sealand. It has been reclaimed as a result of silting up.

The importance of the Great Saughall route, which commenced at that time at Chester Town Hall, was that it ran right through the area later developed as the very large Blacon estate, and thus the Council was able to enhance its services into that development as the houses were built, after the war. As already set out, Blacon itself was not incorporated into Chester until 1936. A timetable dated 9 October 1932 shows that the Saughall route was then operating every 36 minutes.

The other service acquired by Chester also ran out of the city. It too originally commenced at the Town Hall, and continued over the Dee Bridge and through Handbridge before running on to Eccleston Village (Pump). The traffic potential of this route was limited but events were to provide, for a time, far more passengers on it than had been envisaged. One provision of the agreement was that Chester was permitted to run the Eccleston service round via Rake Lane and back to the city via Wrexham Road, but that was never done. The same timetable shows that it was running seven times a day.

Crosville thus retained their services in and through the north-eastern segment of the Chester urban area, which also developed considerably

after the War, leading to the provision of a number of frequent services.

There were some less important provisions. Chester agreed not to operate from the top of Bouverie Street into the lower part of Parkgate Road, thus preserving the local traffic there for Crosville, and Crosville in turn agreed not to run along Whipcord Lane, parallel to Garden Lane, save between South View Road and Gladstone Avenue.

It was agreed that the parties could operate joint services, save in the sector allocated to Crosville, but the only specified such service was a route to Crook O'Dee, a popular fishing spot at Aldford, not far out of Chester, which was never actually introduced.

It was also provided that if in the future the city boundary was extended, that fact could not by itself be used as a ground for overriding the terms of the agreement. It was also agreed that it should endure for eight years in the first instance and thereafter continue unless determined by either party on six months' notice.

This agreement established far more regulated, if not harmonious, relationships between the two main players providing bus services in the city, but it did not lead to a joint operating area as happened in many other places such as Plymouth, and later Southend. Indeed, there were never any joint services at all between Crosville and Chester.

It is not entirely clear whether the two parties thought through what they were signing up to. Once the Traffic Commissioners had been established, it was for them to make decisions about new services. Therefore, had Chester decided that it wanted to apply to run into Hoole, Crosville would have had difficulties relying on the agreement in opposition to such a move, because the terms should have been regarded as unenforceable as in restraint of trade, even apart from the attempted ousting of the jurisdiction of the Commissioners. However, it is an interesting sidelight on the way in which the Commissioners exercised their powers that they were sent a copy of the agreement prior to it being signed, and said that in general it was satisfactory.

On the other hand, the agreement, for example, prevented Chester from providing direct services from its suburbs to the world-famous Zoo, which was squarely within the Crosville sector. The

Council later considered that they had gained from the agreement, but in fact their problem was that they started from a position of weakness because of their prevarication for so many years.

In 1932 the Council was given a licence to run direct services from the General Station to the football ground off Sealand Road, on matchdays and to the nearby greyhound racing track, when meetings were being held; these were not regarded as being in competition with the Crosville stage service.

In September 1932, thus after only a short period of operation, the Eccleston service began running from the General Station rather than from the Town Hall.

In October 1933 the General Station to Cliveden Road service was reorganised so that it became a circular, or more exactly a panhandle, service. Alternate journeys continued on the old route to Cliveden Road via Hough Green, but the other journeys ran via Lache Lane and Circular Drive to reach the terminus. This became a frequent and well-used link, although it does not seem that all journeys then ran round.

In April 1934 some journeys on the Eccleston service were extended the short distance to Eaton Hall, the seat of the Dukes of Westminster and then a very large Victorian mansion, which has since been replaced by a much smaller house. These originally ran only on special occasions and had to use some private estate roads.

Although all these developments to services had taken place, remarkably the fleet had not been further enlarged. This changed in 1934. In June of that year the Council took delivery of two Bedford

Conscious that Chester would soon need more vehicles, AEC arranged for this Q double-decker to visit the undertaking in December 1933. Destined for Grimsby, but acting as a demonstrator, it was 'diverted' from CH Roe in Leeds. In the event the next order for double-deckers would be for Leyland Titans *(BCVM)*

WLBs with 20-seat Duple bodies, which were very unusual vehicles for a municipal operator. They were capable of one-man operation (because of their restricted capacity) and the decision was taken to order them on 26 January 1934, but the minutes do not record the motive behind this odd development. The total cost of the two was £989/10/- and they were supplied by the Chester Engineering Company (1918) Ltd rather than directly by the manufacturer. It may be that they were intended primarily for the Eccleston service, which was Chester's most rural and also required running along the estate drives to reach Eaton Hall.

One of the two small Bedfords is apparently running to Blacon, which in later years required far larger vehicles. *(OS)*

In an interview with Ellis in *Modern Transport* on 29 June 1935 he said that they were for "use on rural and suburban routes at slack times".

The Bedfords were not in the event very successful in service and were both withdrawn after only five years and then used by Chester ARP.

The issue of the use of diesel engines was then put before the Transport Committee. Across the country, these were being introduced and new petrol-engined vehicles, especially double-deckers, were becoming less common.

On 8 March 1934 it was agreed that a diesel-engined vehicle should be hired from Foden of Sandbach, a company which was to play a considerable part in the future operations. At that time Foden were only dipping their toes into bus, as opposed to commercial vehicle, operation. Their only double-deck demonstrator at that time was AMB 834, a DDG6 model which was new in December 1933 with a Burlingham 48-seat body: it is assumed that that was the vehicle used, although it had six cylinders and the minutes say that it was a five-cylinder vehicle. Foden had no such demonstrators at the time. The cost was agreed at 3d per mile. The vehicle had also been demonstrated to Salford earlier in 1934.

The Foden arrived and after the first period it was agreed to prolong the hire and also to hire vehicles from AEC and Crossley. Perhaps surprisingly, it was then decided to buy the Council's first oil-engined bus not from any of

The Foden at Burlingham's Blackpool factory during construction, and after sale to Ebor of Mansfield. No photographs of it in Chester have yet appeared. *(Both Foden/STA)*

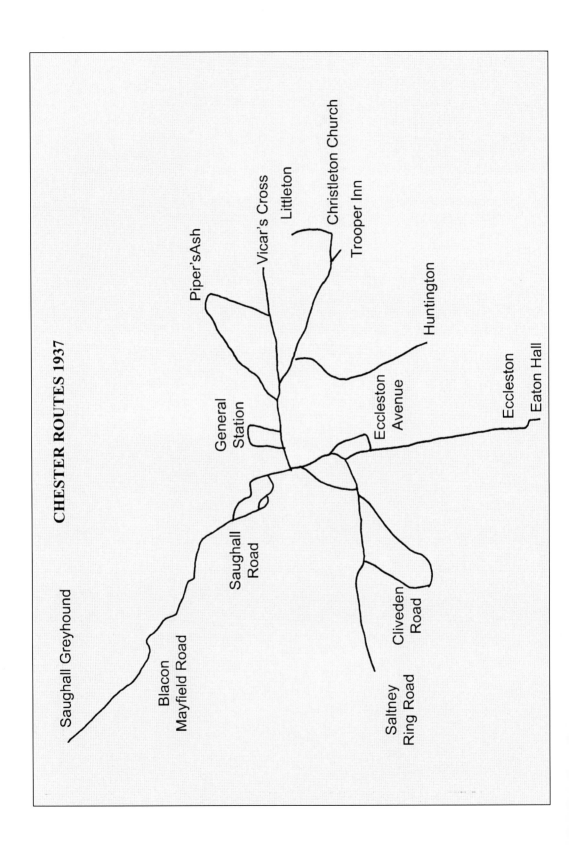

CHESTER ROUTES 1937

Saughall Greyhound

Blacon Mayfield Road

Saughall Road

General Station

Piper'sAsh

Vicar's Cross

Littleton

Christleton Church

Trooper Inn

Huntington

Eccleston Avenue

Eccleston

Eaton Hall

Saltney Ring Road

Cliveden Road

28

these undertakings, but from Leyland. The Foden demonstrator was sold in 1936 to the Ebor Bus Company of Mansfield. However, Fodens would stage a major comeback as we shall see later.

In November 1934 what was, in fact, the first Leyland to be taken into stock was acquired. It was a TD3 with Leyland diesel engine The new Titan had 52-seat body by Massey Bros of Wigan, the first of many vehicles to be supplied to Chester by that company over many years.

No new vehicles arrived in 1935, but attention turned to serving the area of Curzon Park, which was a high-class residential area behind Hough Green. On 4 March 1935 it was agreed that an application be made to divert the service from Christleton Village to Saltney (Anchor) along Selkirk Road, Earlsway and Mount Pleasant, but this was deferred for three months and on 12 March 1935 was abandoned as a proposition because of the number of objections from local residents, who did not want buses running past their homes. In December 1935 a rather crude post card poll was taken of residents of Curzon Park, who voted 2:1 against having a service and the scheme was thus not taken further at that time.

On 30 September 1935 a new service was introduced from the General Station to Blacon, at the junction of Saughall Road with Mayfield Road, which was just within the city boundary. This overlapped with the Town Hall-Great Saughall

Massey-bodied Leyland TD3 (AFM 518) seen at the factory's Enfield Street works prior to delivery. **(Massey/ STA)**

route and reflected increased development of the area even at that time: Mayfield Road was repaired so as to enable double-deckers to turn and thus to be run on the new service, which was then irregular. The Great Saughall service ran about every 40 minutes, as did the Cliveden Road panhandle, in each direction. In the timetable of that date, the General Station to Saughall Road service was shown as running every 30 minutes along Chichester Street (as the Saughall village service did) and every 30 minutes via the old route via Canal Street. There is no record of this dual routing before that date.

It appears that the Leyland/Massey combination had impressed Chester, and a further three vehicles arrived in May 1936. They were on the TD4c chassis, and thus had torque convertors, which led them often to be referred to as "gearless" vehicles, but also had 52-seat Massey bodies. They established a new norm for the operator, in that they had two single-line indicators at the front, the back, and over the entrance, and also a service number indicator at the front. Previous vehicles had had only one single-line indicator and service numbers had not been used.

The issue of service numbers is a complicated one. It would be easy to assume that the delivery of these new vehicles coincided with their introduction but, surprisingly, they are not mentioned at all in the minutes of the Transport Committee. All that can be said with confidence is that they were not in the timetable issued on 15 June 1936, but had been introduced by the time of the timetable which was issued as late as 22 October 1945.

On 15 June 1936 there was a considerable revision of services, which included further expansion of the areas served. Some services from Vicar's Cross to Saltney were extended from West View to Ring Road (now known as Sandy Lane to avoid confusion with the Chester Ring Road), a relatively short distance but thus offering buses to the whole village of Saltney. The Ring Road journeys ran only about hourly, whereas the service to West View was very frequent.

The Saltney (Anchor Hotel) to Christleton Village service was extended from Christleton Church to the nearby rural village of Littleton: initially the service provided was lavish, and on Saturdays ran every 20 minutes.

The two completely new services introduced at this time both broke new ground. They both started at General Station but ran into town not via City Road but by the more northerly route via Brook Street and Frodsham Street. This brought them on to Foregate Street just outside the city walls and slightly further east than the Cross. One

then ran to Dee Banks via Stocks Lane, as the existing service already had done, but continued on to Huntington (Rake & Pikel). The importance of this extension was that in 1938 construction began of a large military establishment, Saighton Camp, which was very near the terminus. It was developed to train anti-aircraft units. Crosville and the Corporation agreed that there would be no objection to this application and reciprocally Chester would not oppose the company's application to the Vickers Armstrong factory at Bretton, near Broughton.

The other new service followed the same route from the station and also turned left (eastwards) on reaching Foregate Street. It then continued along Tarvin Road, but instead of Vicar's Cross it then served Green Lane, which was new territory. Initially this was not run more frequently than hourly and there was a long gap at lunch time.

The Green Lane service retained its original form for only a short time; from 4 January 1937 it became a circular service, running on from its original terminus at the corner with Grove Avenue via Hare Lane through Piper's Ash village and then returning to town via Hoole Lane. This involved

In 1938 Chester took into stock two AEC Regents with the only East Lancs bodies ever bought new. 29 is bound for the Station. Note the revised destination display. *(OS)*

two crossings of the then new Chester Ring Road (A41), which had been constructed in 1935 to start dealing with the traffic congestion which even then was affecting the centre of the city. This at last involved an incursion into Hoole, because the northern part of Hoole Lane was in that district. The great traffic objective on the new extension was the then Chester City Hospital, which was also on Hoole Lane, but nearer the town.

The expansion of the fleet in order to run these new services required further accommodation. There was room to the east of the former horse tramway garage and a new steel framed building was erected. Because of the constraints of space some of the north-eastern corner of the existing building had to be removed. There remained between the old and the new locations a building known as the stables, which reflected its original use. It was used initially as a store and later, after the trams disappeared, as a body shop. Other ancillary buildings were taken into the use of the Transport Department as time went by.

In May 1938 there were yet further alterations, which were driven by the need for additional

Chester No. 32 delivered in 1939 shows the curved frontal profile introduced by East Lancs around this time. It is mounted on an AEC Regent II chassis. *(HSPC)*

journeys to Huntington. The Eccleston Avenue journeys thereafter all ran from General Station, via Brook and Frodsham Streets, and the Huntington service ceased to run across the city. It instead ran from the Town Hall, still via Stocks Lane and Dee Banks, with some journeys ending at Huntington Shops, which were short of the Rake & Pikel. It had to be single-deck operated as it was thought that double-deckers could not be used on the section from Christleton Road down to the river.

In October 1938 Chester took delivery of two further double-deckers. However, there was an about-turn in relation to suppliers of both chassis and body. These were AEC Regents, diesel engined, as opposed to the first ten which had petrol engines, and they had 54-seat bodywork by East Lancashire Coachbuilders, a new supplier; these were the only new bodies by that company ever supplied to the municipality.

On 26 November 1938 the Transport Committee was told that six of the original double-deckers needed replacing forthwith and that the remaining 14 of the 1930 vehicles should be withdrawn within two years. The war was to demonstrate clearly the optimism inherent in that statement.

However, an order was placed for six new double-deckers. It is not at all clear why it was decided to purchase four AECs and two Leylands, instead of concentrating on one manufacturer.

By 1 April 1939 there were 30 vehicles in stock and at that time none had been withdrawn.

In May 1939 the four AEC Regents arrived, also with 54-seat bodies, but this time once again by Massey. The style of body which had by then been adopted by the bodybuilder had a curved frontal profile.

By this time war was very much on the horizon. So far as Chester was concerned, this involved a vast expansion of Saighton Camp, as well as the development of Blacon Camp, on the southern area of that parish, and also the use of parts of Eaton Hall, which were used as a military hospital, and then later housed the Royal Naval College after its premises in Dartmouth were bombed: it then became an Officer Cadets' Training School in 1946.

Both the Saighton and Eaton Hall developments required new services. An additional service to Huntington was instituted in July 1939, using Sandy Lane rather than Stocks Lane and Dee Banks, which enabled double-deckers to run to the Rake & Pikel and thus serve the Camp. Regular services were also instituted to Eaton Hall, instead of the occasional journeys which had been run.

Just before the long-expected war began, Chester took delivery of the two Leylands on order: these were of TD5c specification (thus "gearless" models) with Leyland all-metal 53-seat bodies.

The new deliveries in 1939 enabled some vehicles to be withdrawn. Two of the 1930 Regents went in that year, and the two delivered in 1931. The unsatisfactory small Bedfords were also withdrawn, as already set out.

As well as four AECs, Chester took delivery in 1939 of two Leylands with Leyland bodies. 36 is shown at Leyland's South Works when new. *(OS)*

5: BUS OPERATION 1939-50

The long-expected War finally began on 3rd September 1939. The War had similar effects here as in other places; Chester however escaped bombing.

The Traffic Commissioners were suspended for the period of hostilities and were replaced by a Regional Traffic Commissioner. Relations between Chester and Crosville remained formal and somewhat frosty. By a letter 30 November 1939 the Commissioner recommended that Crosville be able to pick up short-term passengers inwards to the city, but not outwards. Chester saw a clear threat in this and would not agree. The next year the RTC again raised the issue of coordination with Chester but, having not received a favourable response, on 13 April 1940 he decided not to pursue it with Crosville.

Thus, no coordination scheme was imposed on the two parties, as, for example, it effectively was in Plymouth.

In the early stages of the war, services were maintained reasonably well and, for example, it was suggested that the Saughall service should be reduced only from every 45 minutes to every 40 minutes, which was little more than a nominal change. On the other hand, there were continuing problems with the Huntington service and it was reported that local civilians were being crowded out of the buses by the men from Saighton Camp.

At that time also, a limited number of new vehicles were made available which were in the course of construction before the war began. Chester had ordered more batches of double-deckers from both AEC and Leyland, as had been delivered in 1939. On 8 January 1940, AEC told the Council that they could supply three buses immediately, so they resolved to take them and ask Leyland for a further three. The AEC Regents, numbers 37-9, again fitted with 54-seat Massey bodies, arrived in June that year. It took more time before Chester got its Leylands, which arrived between April and June 1941, also with 54-seat Massey bodies. By this time the profile of the front of the Massey bodies had become even more pronounced, and the front pillars were wider: these characteristics were to be found on their post-war productions.

Number 34, an AEC Regent with Massey body, arrived in 1939. It is seen against a typical Chester streetscape with half timbered properties behind and, on the right, the well-known local department store, Browns, which sometimes featured as a timing point. Leylands 35 and 36 completed the 1939 deliveries. *(OS)*

Number 38, the second of the 1940 Regents, amid increased traffic en route for Saltney (Ring Road). *(OS)*

Seen below, 38 is at the Cliveden Road terminus on the then lucrative circular service around the Lache area. *(OS)*

Massey-bodied Leyland TD7, No. 41 was delivered in 1941, again in pursuance of a pre-war order.

On 1 February 1942 there were some minor changes to services. Some journeys on the Vicar's Cross service were curtailed at the Ring Road instead of carrying on the very short distance to the Old Toll Bar. It was decided that all the Saltney services should run via Handbridge, and all Cliveden Road services should run via Grosvenor Bridge and commence from the Town Hall rather than the General Station.

On 8 April 1942 the Transport Committee was told that thereafter new buses could only be obtained with the consent of the Ministry of War Transport and then could only be what they permitted, not necessarily what the customer wanted.

The organisation set up by the Ministry of Supply and the Ministry of War Transport in co-operation with manufacturers and operators in 1941 got to work on specifications for wartime buses while the part-completed vehicles were being allocated. Originally it was planned that there should be initial batches of 500 new double-deckers each from Leyland and Guy, but Leyland were quickly moved to production of tanks, leaving Guy to begin the work.

The general principle was to produce serviceable buses at minimum cost in terms of materials (particularly those in demand for war purposes, notably aluminium) or skilled labour. Standardisation was obviously desirable, and operators were under pressure to accept a common specification.

In 1942 Mr Ellis came to the end of his long tenure as General Manager. He offered to resign on 6 July 1942 but said he would stay on as a consultant, although taking his pension, after 1 October 1942. This was what was done, and for the time being other officers dealt with the day-to-day administrative decisions.

New vehicles were hard to source and, in any event, subject to the strict terms of the utility specification imposed by the Government. Services were curtailed early after 1 February 1943, with no services after 9.30 pm, but were generally very busy because of the absence of other means of transport. The blackout was enforced, making the collection of fares very difficult and increasing the number of accidents. The presence of the military installations also led to very substantial increases in traffic.

Overleaf: This copy of the original drawing of the 'wartime standard normal height double-deck bus' was issued by the National Federation of Vehicle Trades for guidance to bodybuilding concerns. It is undated but shows the original body specification, with steel-panelled emergency exit door, as built from the Autumn of 1941 until late in 1943. Daimler began to build wartime buses almost at the end of 1942.

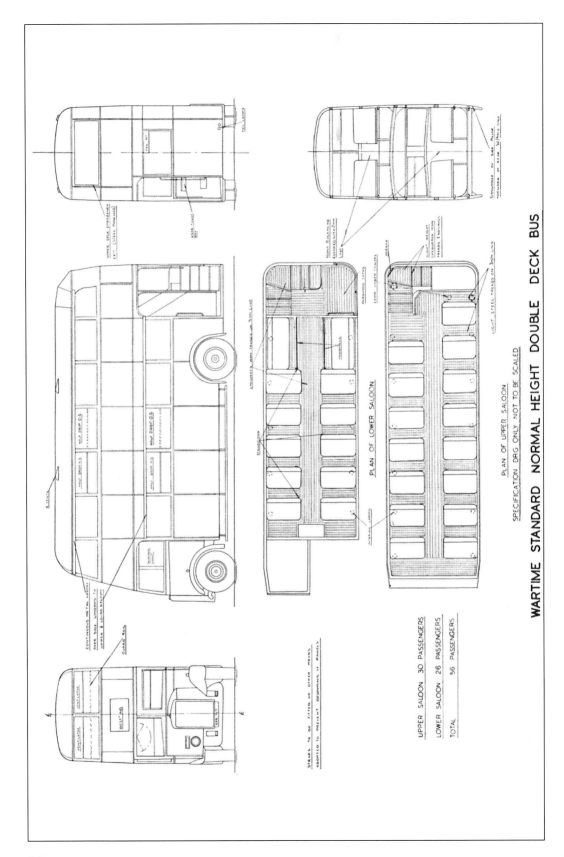

UPPER SALOON   30 PASSENGERS

LOWER SALOON   26 PASSENGERS

TOTAL   56 PASSENGERS

PLAN OF LOWER SALOON

PLAN OF UPPER SALOON

SPECIFICATION DRG ONLY NOT TO BE SCALED

WARTIME STANDARD NORMAL HEIGHT DOUBLE DECK BUS

In September 1942 Chester took delivery of its first two vehicles to full utility specification. There was no question of being able to choose the make of vehicle by then: they were five-cylinder Guy Arab Is with 56-seat Massey bodies to the prescribed spartan pattern, which included a reversion to single-line destination indicators.

There was another minor change with effect from 12 October 1942, when buses were diverted so as not to serve Piper's Ash village, which thereafter could only be reached from the stop at the corner of Hoole Lane and the Ring Road. This deviation meant that the circular service did not have to cross the Ring Road, but rather ran along a short portion of it.

Although Chester had taken delivery of a number of new vehicles in the late 1930s, their remaining elderly AECs were not fit for further service, as had been envisaged in 1938, particularly, of course, in the enforced hard conditions. From 1943 onwards the remaining original Regents were taken out of service: five of the Regals were still in service when peace returned. The first four of the gearless Leylands lasted only until 1945.

On 1 February 1943 there was a further minor cut-back in the network. The Littleton section was abandoned for the time being.

1943 did, however, see the arrival of no fewer than six new utility double-deckers, numbered 45-50, all with 56-seat bodies. In June a Daimler CWG5 with Massey bodywork was taken into service, followed in August by a Guy Arab II bodied by Duple. In November four Daimlers to CWA6 specification came into service, all with Duple bodies.

From 1944, as the tide of war began to change in favour of the Allied forces, there was a gradual relaxation of the ban on late services and reinstatement of those which had been axed. That year also saw no fewer than eight new double-deckers taken into stock; clearly this was a reflection of the military presence in the area and the need to provide adequate reliable transport. In March another Guy Arab II with Massey bodywork arrived, followed in May by another four to similar specification. In November three more Daimler CWA6s came, but this time with Brush bodies. In January 1945 the last of this batch came. Chester, as with

45 was a Daimler CWG5 with Massey body to utility specification, delivered in 1943. It was pictured on the Eaton Hall service, which then required double-deckers. *(OS)*

many other places, ended the war with a run-down and worn-out fleet, but proportionately they had taken delivery of more vehicles than many similar municipal operators.

Chester had also employed conductresses during the war, but unlike in many other places they were not dismissed when the men came back after discharge. The Council continued to employ both men and women in that capacity until one-person operation became the norm. Much later, on 12 November 1956, a stern warning was issued that conductresses should wear either berets or uniform hats on their head, but nothing else.

With the arrival of peace, there was an enormous desire to go out to the cinema and other entertainments, and despite the very difficult economic conditions the local authority was anxious to continue its development of the network. The need for utility specifications ended, but the next few years saw an unprecedented demand for new vehicles as operators attempted to rebuild their fleets and in particular to restock coaches as those who had struggled for so long began to travel again. One consequence of this was that many new firms began building bus and coach bodies, and the combination of a lack of expertise and the widespread use of unseasoned timber led to many problems across the country.

The Arab II was designed to accommodate either the five-cylinder 5LW, or six-cylinder 6LW engine and is recognisable by the protruding radiator. Number 46, a Guy Arab II with Duple utility body arrived in 1943. It is seen in original condition outside the Queen Hotel, near the General Station, on a Races special. It was later given a new Massey body. *(OS)*

After the continuity which had been a clear feature of the administration of the municipal undertaking for many years, the immediate post-war years saw a number of changes. After Mr Ellis' final and complete retirement, on 16 April 1945 eight candidates for the post of General Manager were interviewed. The successful applicant was Lee Wilkes, who came from the small Darwen undertaking. His salary was fixed at £650 per annum.

The pressure for new facilities began immediately. On 10 September 1945 Chester were asked to operate to Broughton, the other side of Saltney, and replied that it was out of its area. It was also asked to increase the services to Huntington, which had been a problem throughout the war.

The first post-war timetable was issued on 22 October 1945 and displayed route numbers. The services then operated were:

1. Town Hall-Saughall Road-Blacon (Mayfield Road);
2. Town Hall-Saughall Road-Blacon-Great Saughall;
3. Town Hall-Cross-Huntington (Rake & Pikel) via Dee Banks;
4. Town Hall-Cross-Huntington (Rake & Pikel) via Sandy Lane;
6. Saltney (West View and Anchor)-Cross-Christleton (Trooper Inn);
7/8. Town Hall-Cross-Cliveden Road circular;
9. General Station-Cross-Eccleston Village;
10. General Station-Cross-Eccleston-Eaton Hall, some journeys on which were numbered 29;
14. General Station-Cross-Eccleston Avenue;
20. General Station-Town Hall-Saughall Road (all via Chichester Street);
23. Saltney (Anchor)-Cross-Christleton Church;
25. Saltney (Ring Road, West View and Anchor)-Cross-Vicar's Cross (Ring Road);
26. Saltney (West View and Anchor)-Cross-Vicar's Cross (Ring Road and Old Toll Bar).

Some other numbers were allocated throughout to odd journeys, particularly to and from the Station, which were in fact running to or from the garage.

On 3 December 1945 the Transport Committee decided that all of the service to Huntington should run via Sandy Lane, so that double-deckers could maintain the whole service, and the Stocks Lane section could be abandoned. This came into effect from 11 March 1946, but there was a rowing back from the relinquishment of the initial route and some journeys running only to Huntington Shops (short of the Rake & Pikel) via Stocks Lane were retained (service 3), but only between 9 and 12 and then in the afternoon between 2 and 5. Single-deckers continued to be used on what was regarded as a shopping service, and since it did not reach Saighton Camp it was not crowded out by servicemen. This eventually commenced running on 8 July 1946.

During the war, Crosville had given up running local buses on Parkgate Road, which, of course, had formed part of the 1932 agreement. On 11 March 1946 Wilkes reported that he had applied to the RTC (who was still in place at that time) to operate from Parkgate Road (Woodlands Avenue), which was beyond the railway bridge where Chester had run from 1930 to 1932, via the city and Curzon Park to Saltney (Mount Pleasant), the latter portion of which had been proposed before the war. Crosville said that they would oppose this, but on 8 April 1946 they applied to reinstate their local service on Parkgate Road (on which they had said there was insufficient traffic available) and Chester then decided it did not want to proceed with its existing application, but would rather seek a new service from the General Station via St Anne's Street, the centre of the Newtown area, which had never been served, through the city and then via Curzon Park to Mount Pleasant and Saltney.

All was not straight forward, however. The General Manager was not afraid of giving his views and on 13 March 1946 he suggested that the Grove Avenue service should run only via Hoole Lane and that the Tarvin Road section, much of which was served by buses to Vicar's Cross, should be abandoned. This, however, was not carried through.

There was an important change at this time to the appearance of the Corporation's vehicles. In January 1946 the Transport Committee gave consideration to the decision by Crosville, now under Tilling control, to abandon their traditional maroon livery and instead to use green. At that time, it was resolved that the municipal buses should be painted green all over "of a shade different from that now used by the Crosville company", so prospective passengers would be able to distinguish their vehicles.

However, Crosville then vacillated about the exact shade they were going to use, and the Transport Manager reported to the 11 March meeting that his counterpart had reported that for the next few years vehicles "of every shade of green" would run in service from Crane Wharf. By coincidence, at this meeting the Committee also inspected a Foden double-decker bus on demonstration, and were impressed by its maroon and cream livery. This was HMB 395, a PVD6 with Willowbrook lowbridge body, which in due course passed to Warrington Corporation, which had it rebodied.

The consequence was that it was resolved "that the buses be painted maroon and cream similar to the Foden test vehicle". Thus, in effect the two local rivals exchanged liveries. In the interim, many Chester vehicles had maroon stripes painted on them until they were fully repainted. The maroon and cream thus adopted was impressive and dignified. The minutes of the Transport Committee make it entirely clear that the oft-told story of the adoption of this livery was not a myth.

Wilkes' time in Chester was, however, short. On 26 June 1946 he tendered his resignation in order to take up an equivalent position with Newport Corporation.

During the war, no new single-deckers had been taken into stock and the only such vehicles still in stock were the remaining original AEC Regals of 1930. They were withdrawn in 1946 and 1947, and in the case of the last of them, 1949.

In June 1946 two new single-deckers arrived. They were also AEC Regals, but had Massey 32-seat bodies fitted with front entrances. They had half-canopy bodies with single-line destination indicators both over the cab and over the recessed canopy. They were to have very long lives in the city although they had an old-fashioned appearance even when new: see page 43.

On 26 July 1946 another meeting was held to decide who should succeed Wilkes. The candidates included HJ Hooley, who was then in

Number 53 was a Guy Arab II, originally with Massey utility body, which by the time of the photograph had been rebodied by DJ Davies. It was on a 9 journey to Eccleston Avenue and was caught at the General Station. *(OS)*

Burton but was later to play an important part in the history of Chester Transport. However, on this occasion he was not appointed and the successful applicant was EG Thomas, who had previously worked for Merthyr.

On 7 October 1946 it was agreed by the committee to apply for the Vicar's Cross service to be extended just over a mile along the main A51 road to the junction of the road to Guilden Sutton, which was a considerable length of new route.

While that was pending, the arrival of the new single-deckers enabled the Council finally to inaugurate the Curzon Park service. After the Station and Newtown, it served the area of Delamere Street, the location of the main Crosville terminus in the city, the Town Hall and then ran via Dee Bridge and Handbridge to Hough Green, round Curzon Park and along Mount Pleasant to Saltney, but no further than the Anchor. There were high hopes for this service, but, in fact, the traffic potential was never high and it did not ever run more frequently than hourly. Another route with limited traffic potential was the single-deck service to Christleton Church.

It is interesting that in both 1945 and 1946 proper timetable books were issued with the journeys set out in conventional form, which

was easy to follow. It was also the case that the development of the Blacon area had started, but initially it was over-provided with journeys. In 1946 the 1 ran every 20 minutes and the 2 every 40 minutes. The overlapping 20 was by post-war years reduced to running every 30 minutes. On the other hand, the Huntington service was generally every 15 to 20 minutes, but in rush hours ran every 5 minutes, to cope with the military personnel.

The new General Manager applied his mind to the problems caused by two of the single-deck services and with effect from 8 April 1947 the service from Saltney to Christleton Village (23) and the service to Huntington Shops via Stocks Lane (3) were both abandoned; services continued to run from Saltney to the Trooper Inn. The two services which were given up were replaced by new links. The journeys from General Station via St Anne Street were diverted after the Town Hall to run to Christleton Church, but left the main road to serve Stocks Lane, Beckett's Lane and Heath Lane, thus providing a more regular replacement for the Dee Banks journeys. These were numbered 23A. At the same time, the journeys from Curzon Park ceased to run to Saltney and instead ran along Park Road West and Earlsway, returning via Selkirk Road. They too then ran to Christleton Church via the Stocks Lane diversion and became the 23. There were adjustments to the Saughall Road provision: too many journeys had been provided, and the 1 and

At the Town Hall, 57 loads for Saughall. A Daimler with Brush utility body, it was in the intermediate livery with maroon bands painted on. Note the shallow ventilation windows at the front of the upper-deck as shown on the official general arrangement drawing. Massey did not fit these on Chester's vehicles. *(OS)*

The last utility-bodied vehicle taken into stock was 59, another Daimler with Brush body delivered in 1945 and also showing additional stripes of maroon. *(OS)*

55 was another utility Guy Arab, but it was rebodied in 1952 by Massey. It was on Races special duties. *(OS)*

2 ran every 40 minutes each, with a combined frequency to Mayfield Road of every 20 minutes. Correspondingly, the 20 was increased to run every 15 minutes, a late flourish for a service which thereafter was to wither.

The Traffic Commissioners, who had earlier indicated that they would approve of the extension to Guilden Sutton Lane End, then said that they would not approve it as a terminus because of the difficulty of turning there. They suggested that Littleton Lane be used instead, but that would not have met the perceived need for a long extension. The mood was clearly in favour of meeting the huge demand which existed. Eaton Hall had had frequent services during the war and in its new capacity as a Cadets' Training School needed more.

Chester was then asked to extend its services to Saighton Village because the Crosville service was said to be inadequate, but an application for that would have fractured the truce between the two operators. It was suggested that all the West View services should be extended to the Ring Road (Sandy Lane), but that was regarded as unnecessary. At this time there was a bus to West View every five minutes.

The complaint about Crosville was not isolated and indeed it was having grave difficulty meeting the needs of the villages around Chester. On 8 November 1948 Chester was presented with a petition from local residents asking for the Christleton Village and the Trooper Inn services to be joined to make a circular through Rowton and Waverton. Initially Thomas said he would apply for permission to run this, but he then met a representative of Crosville, who agreed to operate further buses to the area, so no action was taken by the Council.

The year 1947 saw the arrival of substantial reinforcements to the fleet. Perhaps influenced by their experience of the utility vehicles, Chester purchased six more Daimlers. There were grave delays and shortages at this time and in fact the six vehicles which arrived were both late and represented a temporary shortfall. In 1945 Chester had ordered four double-deck vehicles with Daimler engines. Three of these arrived in July or August 1947 and are recorded by the manufacturer as still being designated CWD6, in other words with W for war as opposed to V for victory. In the following year, 1946, they ordered a further four double-deck Daimlers, but this time with AEC engines. Again, only three arrived initially, the first two

Number 65 was one of the two AEC Regals with Massey half-cab bodies which were the first non-utility vehicles taken into the fleet. It was in the familiar Town Hall area. *(OS)*

in May, before the earlier order. These were designated as CVA6 models, ie with 6 cylinders.

All these Daimlers were supposed to have Metro-Cammell bodies but because of delays the order was moved to Massey. The Metro-Cammell body order was diverted to Salford Corporation, which was attempting to reinvigorate its fleet from an unprecedented state of decrepitude at the end of the war, under the direction of its charismatic new manager, Charles Baroth.

The remaining two Daimlers from these two orders were not delivered until February 1948, and again had Massey 56-seat bodies. Massey provided D-shaped windows at the ends of the lower deck, which were characteristic of their output at the time.

In addition to all these double-deckers, in October 1947 two further AEC Regal single-deckers, similar to those which had arrived the year before, came to Chester. Thus, the by then small single-deck fleet was comprehensively renewed. Another welcome development was the decision to replace the wooden seating on the utility vehicles with moquette. Initially seats from buses which were being withdrawn were used for this purpose.

One of the diverted Daimlers became a celebrity when it was exhibited by Daimler at the World's Fair in Copenhagen in 1948. Mr Baroth poses with the vehicle and the four crew members before setting off. CRJ 343 carried a GB plate for the rest of its life in Salford. *(STA)*

43

Two more Regals with Massey bodies, which looked antiquated even when new, arrived in 1947. 69 is waiting to leave for Christleton. *(OS)*

Another of the 1945 order for Massey-bodied Daimlers was 66, inward bound from Eccleston Avenue to the Station. *(OS)*

The slatted wooden seat was part of the specification of all types of British wartime bus from the latter part of 1943, and buses continued to be built to similar design until early 1945. This is the upper-deck of the Brush-bodied Daimler CWA6. Forward vision was adversely affected by the heavy frames of the hinged vents over the forward-facing windows. Note that only one window opened on each side and the single-skin side and roof, the framework of the latter a hazard to heads of unwary passengers.

The lower-deck view of the same vehicle conveys typical standards of wartime interior finish, Brush being perhaps marginally better than most. Although seeming very spartan by modern standards, slatted seats had been used on tramcars of many undertakings up to the late 'twenties and many were still in service until after the 1939-45 war. *(Massey/STA)*

On 2 August 1948 there was a short extension to the new General Station-Christleton service from the Church to the Girls' School; the canal bridge had still not been rebuilt, so this was still restricted to single-deckers. At that stage the Curzon Park service still ran only to the Church, but on 13 December 1948 four journeys a day on that route were extended to Littleton, restoring a link which had been cut in the war, albeit at a much-reduced level. However, the Littleton journeys (only) ran via the Grosvenor Bridge rather than Handbridge, in order to adjust the schedules, which was an unnecessary complication.

The Golf Club at Vicar's Cross, which was near but not quite as far out as the Lane End, agreed to provide a turning point on its land and that application too was granted on 2 August. Services to the Golf Club ran only from the city centre. This turned out to be a very unremunerative section and this was reported as early as 7 February 1949.

In November 1948 Chester took delivery of the first of what was to prove a fleet of ten Foden double-deckers, eight of which had Massey bodies. The first order was for five, and the records do not reveal whether other tenders were sought.

The 1945 order for Daimlers did not begin to arrive until 1947: 63 had the familiar Massey body and is outside the Cathedral. *(OS)*

Number 60 was part of a delayed order to revive the fleet after the war. It was a Daimler CVA6 with Massey body and is bound for Vicar's Cross (Ring Road), just short of the normal terminus. *(OS)*

Fodens had constructed very few passenger vehicles before the war, one of which had, of course, been demonstrated then to Chester, but in 1945 they decided to make a serious attempt to break into the bus market. The first chassis so developed was the PVD6, as shown by the demonstrator the livery of which had so impressed the Transport Committee. Fodens had the advantage to Chester of being manufactured locally, at Sandbach, which meant that they could attend easily if required. The new chassis was revolutionary in that it had a full bonnet rather than an exposed radiator, and one selling-point was the ease of removing the whole engine in order to carry out work to it. This first Foden, JFM 745, had been exhibited at the 1948 Commercial Motor Show and so had been finished by Massey to a very high standard, including especially good quality moquette seating. Director JE Foden came with this bus to hand it over in November 1948. There was no extra charge for the special features incorporated into the vehicle; the catalogue for the Show indicated that the cost complete was £4,131.

Fodens wanted Birmingham, Liverpool, Manchester and other such large fleets to take their vehicles. That did not happen and the major municipalities continued to order from those manufacturers which they had always used, although Guy also acquired many sales across the country because their vehicles had proved so reliable after being supplied during the war, when there was no choice. Only about 60 double-deckers were sold by Foden, and the largest number (15) went to Warrington, also local to the factory. Chester had the second largest number, and five were supplied to Derby and to Lancashire United as well as penny numbers to others. They were far more successful with their single-deckers and especially with coaches, because the demand was so high. They then pioneered a rear-engineered single-deck coach but it was too far ahead of its time.

Foden double-deckers seem to have been generally mechanically reliable in service although some were handicapped by the bodywork fitted. Merthyr Tydfil was particularly unfortunate in having its vehicles bodied by Welsh Metal Industries, which became a byword for problems and in particular water ingress. Chester, of course, usually used Massey, so the bodywork was of a high standard and lasted well.

The first and later Fodens for Chester dispensed with the destination indicator over the platform but had one at the rear. The balance of the first order for Fodens was a further four, which arrived in March 1949.

In July 1949 the annual guide by Philipson & Golder to local train and bus services was published, which well demonstrates the routes run by both Chester and Crosville in the city. There was no Chester Corporation timetable at that time. The Chester network, which in principle was quite simple, was beginning to show the complications and variations which plagued it in later years.

Pictured at the 1948 Commercial Motor Show in London is Chester Corporation's No. 72, a Foden PVD6, price 'complete as shown £4,131', as stated in the catalogue. This vehicle was the first of a batch of eight with typical Massey body styling of that period. *(Massey/STA)*

Testimonials to Foden Craftsmanship are to be found in Cities, Towns and Villages of the British Isles

NO OTHER NAME MEANS QUITE THE SAME

FODENS LIMITED, SANDBACH · CHESHIRE · ENGLAND   Britain's Leading Builders of Road Transport Vehicles

Telephones : Sandbach 44 (6 lines)   Telegrams : " Fodenway " Sandbach

The first Foden in the fleet was 72, which arrived in 1948 after being shown at the Commercial Motor Show. It was running to Blacon (Stamford Road) from the Town Hall. *(OS)*

The second Foden was 73, one of 4 which arrived in 1949. It is shown parked on a corner before leaving the city: a small child seems daunted by the platform. *(OS)*

A summary of the services operated at that time is as follows, the frequencies being for the general Monday to Friday daytime:

1. Town Hall-Saughall Road-Blacon (Mayfield Road). Every 10 minutes, including the journeys on service 2, with a few shorter runs to Blacon Lodge.
2. Town Hall-Saughall Road-Blacon (Mayfield Road)-Great Saughall (Greyhound Inn). Every 40 minutes.
3. Town Hall-Sandy Lane-Huntington (Rake & Pikel). Every 15 to 20 minutes.
6. Saltney (Ring Road or West View)-City Centre-Christleton (Trooper Inn). About every 12 to 15 minutes from West View and about hourly from Ring Road.
7. Town Hall-Cliveden Road, out via Hough Green, in via Lache Lane. About every 15 to 20 minutes.
8. Reverse of 7 at similar frequency.
10. General Station-City Centre-Eccleston-Eaton Hall. 14 journeys, most to Eaton Hall.
11. General Station-City Centre-Hoole Lane-Piper's Ash-Green Lane. Variable frequency from every 20 minutes to hourly. Continues as 12.
12. General Station-City Centre-Green Lane. Frequency as 11 and continues as 11.
14. General Station-City Centre-Handbridge (Eccleston Avenue). Every 15 minutes.
20. As service 1 but extended from General Station, with extras to Great Saughall. About every 15 minutes.
23. Curzon Park-City Centre-Heath Lane-Christleton-Littleton. Hourly.
23A. General Station-St Anne Street-City Centre-Heath Lane-Christleton (Girls' School). Hourly.
26/29. Saltney (Ring Road or West View)-City Centre-Vicar's Cross. Every 12 to 15 minutes from West View and about hourly from Ring Road. Some journeys were curtailed at Vicar's Cross (Ring Road) and the chart has the memorable note: RR-from Ring Road to Ring Road.

In addition, there were 5 unnumbered journeys from the City Centre to Vicar's Cross Golf Club, and there were other odd journeys from the General Station, or in other words the garage, to Christleton Road (Trooper Inn) (5), Saltney (18), and Vicars Cross (21).

The local services being run by Crosville in Chester at this time are also of importance. They were as follows:

Chester-Hoole circular service. Every 10 to every 20 minutes.
General Railway Station-City Centre-Sealand Road (Blacon Point). Hourly with some extras.
Chester-The Bache-Upton-by-Chester: Seven buses an hour, one of which ran on as a circular back to Chester.
Chester-Piper's Ash circle, in one direction via Hoole Lane. Every 30 minutes each way.

The last was a clear rival to the Council, as it too ran along Hoole Lane with the 11/12 circle. Crosville also served Christleton, on some journeys to Tattenhall, and Saughall, on a few journeys to Shotton and Deeside; an occasional one even ran through Blacon. However, the 1932 agreement restricted their picking up on these and the number of vehicles used for these shorter services was dwarfed by those required for the very frequent routes to Birkenhead, Ellesmere Port and Warrington.

A new variation introduced shortly after this was that most of the journeys on the Great Saughall service, instead of the shorter journeys to Blacon, were extended to the General Station via City Road. Then on 17 November 1949 the Vicar's Cross Golf Club journeys were abandoned after a short life. All services thereafter turned at the top of Littleton Lane, which was itself not regarded as entirely suitable. On the same day three buses a day commenced running from the Town Hall to Blacon Camp via Hillside Road; this was after a request by the Commander of the establishment and the route included use of what was then a private road owned by the War Department.

Blacon was continuing to develop and services were frequently increased. One of the problems was that the only access at this time to the new estate was via the side streets off Parkgate Road, which thus had to carry more heavy traffic than was appropriate.

Chester was obviously satisfied with its Fodens and on 11 July 1949 it was resolved that a further five be obtained, with expected delivery in April 1951. Then on 26 September 1949 it was decided that moquette should be purchased to deal with the nine buses which still carried wooden seating. Many of the replaced wooden seats were sold to the Zoo for the use of visitors.

The year 1950 saw over 16,500,000 passengers carried on the system, which was the highest ever, and this landmark was reached much earlier here than in many other places.

6: BUS OPERATION 1950-59

There was a short respite in the development of new services after 1950, until building in the Blacon area began proceeding with yet more vigour. However, there was a subtle change to the network in that in January 1950 the direction of the loop to Eccleston Avenue was reversed, but instead of returning via the main Eaton Road the buses used Eaton Avenue and Appleyard's Lane, where the terminus was established. On those buses running through to Eaton Hall, the destination was also altered to "Officer Cadet School via Eccleston", because members of the public had been riding on them into the private grounds of the house.

The short service 20 journeys to Saughall Road (Canal Bridge) were reduced in number and more services ran through to Blacon itself. This led to complaints that prospective passengers on the inner section could not board the buses as they were already full, but by 1951 nearly all journeys ran at least as far as Blacon Station.

Two Fodens from the 1949 order arrived in November and December 1950, with the usual Massey bodies, and were registered as MFM 556 and 557. They were to prove entirely satisfactory.

The first of the 1950 repeat order for Massey-bodied Fodens was 77, which was here bound for the General Station. *(TL/PH)*

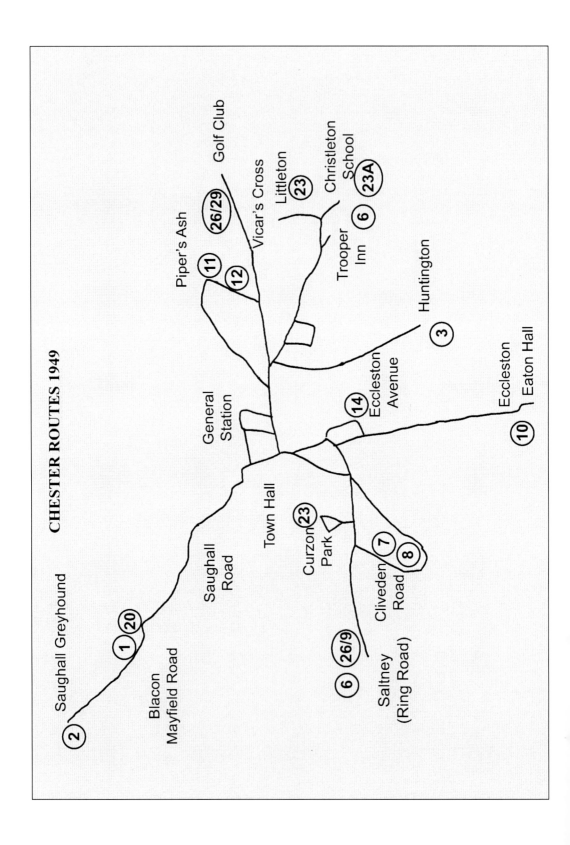

CHESTER ROUTES 1949

Outside the Cathedral was 79, one of the two Fodens delivered in 1951 with ill-fated bodywork by DJ Davies. *(OS)*

The other Davies-bodied Foden was 80, seen by the steps up to the Town Hall on a Football Special to Sealand Road. *(OS)*

In early 1951 two more Fodens came to Chester and they were registered as MFM 634 and 635. They were, however, bodied not by Massey but by DJ Davies of Merthyr Tydfil. It is not clear why the body order was split, because the prices quoted by the two bodybuilders were almost identical. The styling by both suppliers was similar, and all the Fodens from both sources had D-shaped windows at the end of the lower deck.

The eponymous David John Davies was a businessman with his fingers in many pies in Merthyr, where he was universally known as "Sharkey": he ran a bus service of his own, Wheatsheaf Motors, was a local agent for Dennis, had a shop selling electrical and other equipment in the town, and was one of the leading backers of the local football team, which enjoyed huge success after the war in the Southern League. He was a consummate salesman, but the goods supplied did not always arrive on time or match up to expectations. This turned out to be the case with these bodies, which had a much shorter life than those supplied by Massey. It may be the cause of the South Wales bodybuilder was advanced by the Manager, who, of course, had served in Merthyr as deputy to the Superintendent there, and must have known the ubiquitous Davies.

It seems that the order for five Fodens had been reduced at some point to four, with the bodybuilding contract split equally between Massey and Davies. All four had thus been delivered by March 1951.

However, a fifth Foden did appear. The contemporary documentation shows very clearly that this vehicle, which was registered as OFM 33, was offered to Chester in about June 1951 by Massey Brothers, who said that the order for it had been cancelled by "a private operator".

The origins of this vehicle are tangled, and very unclear despite considerable research. In 1949 two identical Massey-bodied Foden double-deckers were delivered to local operators. The first, FDM 568, went to P & O Lloyd of Bagillt, not far away in North Wales, who ran contract services. The other, FDM 724, went to their near neighbours Phillips of Holywell, who ran a stage service, and coincidentally also bought one of Chester's original 1930 AEC Regals when it was withdrawn. It is clear that Lloyds had ordered a second, identical, vehicle. The Foden records suggest that the chassis of MFM 556 had originally been intended for Lloyds: it may be that they vacillated after placing the original

order and certainly at this time they took a number of second-hand double-deckers for their factory services. Both the Fodens delivered to Chester in 1950 had bodies finished by Massey to Chester standards and certainly by the time MFM 556 ended up at the bodybuilders, it had ceased to have any connection with Lloyds.

The problems really appear with OFM 33. It had a Massey contract number dating from 1949, which was very near to those attributed to the two other Fodens for North Wales, which had consecutive body numbers, but a Foden chassis number consistent with it being built in 1951. The Massey number tends to suggest that the order was placed with them in 1949. There is no doubt that, whenever the contract number was dated, the body actually put on the vehicle was constructed in 1951 and was to Chester's usual standards. The two Fodens for the North Wales operators had upper-deck windows which differed from those supplied to Chester and the destination displays were of another pattern.

The final Foden was Massey-bodied 81, which has mystery attached to its origin as described in the text. It was pictured coming in to the city from Handbridge en route for Vicar's Cross. *(OS)*

The numbering restarted in 1953 with the delivery of Guy Arab IV/Massey 1, the first of many and itself later preserved. *(OS)*

Number 1, resplendent in preservation. *(JAS)*

It is possible that Lloyds decided to revive their order in 1951, but then had cold feet after the chassis had gone to Massey. They did not fall out with them and sent other new double-deckers to them to be bodied later in the decade. The alternative is that another, unknown, independent operator had an unrecorded order which they cancelled. Certainly, the Chester minutes strongly suggest that OFM 33 was an "extra" bus and was not the fifth of the original order, but the sequence of events is not at all clear. The full truth is now lost in the mysteries of time.

OFM 33 was to be the last of the Foden marque supplied to Chester, although Warrington persisted and took delivery of more vehicles between 1954 and 1956. It is not clear why there were no further orders from Chester to this source.

Pressure continued to be put on the undertaking to take over some areas from Crosville. On 11 September 1950 Chester was again asked to extend services to Broughton; the answer was in the negative but it was indicated that consideration would be given to extending to the new Mainwaring Estate, which was being constructed in Saltney to the south of the main road.

On 20 August 1951 the circular service to Cliveden ceased to operate, as an experiment. There was an overlapping section, as the Lache Lane journeys (8) continued up to Cliveden Road shops, where there was a small roundabout. The Hough Green journeys (7) ran down to the corner of Cliveden Road and Circular Drive. They were shortly extended to the junction of Circular Drive and Green Lane, along a previously unserved road, but this proved uneconomic and on 24 March 1952 the circular services were reintroduced.

The traffic problems which were increasingly to plague Chester had begun to affect the city even as early as 1950. On 20 August 1951 the first of a number of one-way systems was introduced, which made part of Eastgate Street one-way westwards; additional mileage was needed for buses travelling eastwards, which were diverted via Northgate Street and then St Werburgh Street, past the Cathedral and also serving the Town Hall.

The Town Hall is in the background of 4, one of the three Guy Arab IVs delivered with unusual four bay Guy/Park Royal bodies. It is bound for the Station. *(OS)*

It was also decided at this time to have some of the wartime utility Guys rebodied, in order to prolong their life. None of the Daimlers were so treated, and indeed not all of the Guys. In 1952 two of the 1944 Arabs were rebodied by DJ Davies, and although there were not the problems with these as occurred with the Fodens, they did not have the same very long life thereafter as did those who were rebodied by Massey. Massey treated another of the 1944 Arabs in 1952, and the single 1943 Arab in 1953. The rebodying programme here was limited in scope compared with that in some other places.

The development of Blacon was proceeding apace at this time. In July 1951 the Transport Committee agreed that they would all visit the area to consider how it could best be served. The underlying problem, which was never addressed, was that one branch of the City Council was overseeing the construction of this very substantial housing estate, without giving any consideration as to how another branch of the same Council could access and serve it with buses: at that time nearly everyone living there would have had no recourse to a car. This was noted at a meeting of the Transport Committee on 16 November 1951, when it was told that Highfield Road needed a service as housing continued to be built, but that it was too narrow for buses to be used.

In October 1951 the Department was shocked by Thomas' sudden death. It was necessary to interview for a prospective manager yet again. On this occasion Hooley was not interviewed and the successful applicant was W Astin, who came from Colchester.

From 13 October 1952 extra journeys were instituted to the corner of Blacon Avenue and Stamford Road, one of the many termini on the estate which were used; Stamford Road was at first referred to only as Road Number 1. The eastern side of the area was also being covered with houses, and a serious problem was posed for it by the bridge over Blacon Hall Road, which carried the railway line from Northgate Station on to Blacon Station and then to Connah's Quay. The bridge was too low for the operation of double-deckers, and to serve the area from the western end involved a long diversion. On the same date a new service was begun from the Town Hall to Blacon (Ludlow Road) via Blacon Hall Road, which was restricted to the few single-deckers which the undertaking

ran. This initially ran every 30 minutes. This series of changes also finally brought about the end of the pioneering short service to the Canal Bridge on Saughall Road. It also introduced a period in which the Great Saughall service, with its rural section, ran every 20 minutes, the best frequency it ever had. Some locals asked for it to be extended about a quarter of a mile further into the village, but this was not accepted.

There was a renumbering of services with effect from 15 February 1953. Thereafter, all services from General Station to Blacon and Great Saughall, including the journeys to Blacon Camp, were numbered 1. The new single-deck service to Ludlow Road was numbered 2. General Station to Christleton Girls' School was renumbered to 3, and Curzon Park to Littleton became 4. The Saltney services became 5 (to Christleton (Trooper Inn)) and 6 (to Vicar's Cross). General Station to Eccleston Avenue became 9, and to Eccleston Village and Eaton Hall 10. The Town Hall to Huntington service became 13. The Cliveden circulars remained as 7 and 8 and the Green Lane circulars as 11 and 12. The result was much tidier, but as the years went by more and more variations were introduced.

The timetable reflecting these changes also modified the very generous service to Saughall. Thereafter there were buses every 30 minutes to each of Great Saughall, to Stamford Road, both on 1, and to Ludlow Road on 2. This involved a consequential reduction in the number of services being run to Mayfield Road. By this time the service to Saltney Ring Road had also been improved to half hourly. A proper timetable booklet was still being produced at this time.

In 1953 further new vehicles were required. The pre-war double-deckers were being withdrawn and the fleet was continuing to require about 50 vehicles. However, and although Foden was still prepared to build double-deckers, as Warrington's example opposite, showed, Chester turned to Guy, and were in the event to prove one of the most loyal of that company's supporters. Three new Guy Arab IVs with exposed radiators and the customary Massey 56-seat bodies arrived in June and July 1953: numbers had by then reached 81 (the last Foden) and the Arabs started again at 1, as all the original low-numbered vehicles had long since disappeared. As with the Fodens, they were all powered by 6-cylinder engines.

There were more problems by this time with accommodating the vehicles. The fleet had comprised 30 buses in 1939, then 36 in 1947, but had reached 50 by 1950, as the council reacted to the growth of new areas and the pent-up demand which was released after the war.

In 1953 it was decided that the garage needed further extension. The former Manager's house on the garage site was known as Transport House and had just been offered to a driver, as by this time Managers did not want to live on the premises, unless forced to; Wilkes had lived there for a short time when first appointed, but only until he found somewhere else. It was suggested that the garden and lawn at the back of the house be adapted, together with perhaps the paddock of the ambulance station. On 27 January 1954 the Council, unhelpfully, said that no new building should be erected at that time, but the ground could be taken and adapted, and that part of the scheme then proceeded. It was then decided to adapt Transport House as a store for the depot, and to provide in it a lavatory block for the conductresses.

The owner of this preserved Warrington Foden, a rare example of the make commented ruefully on the extremely heavy steering. A possible reason for avoidance in big city mixed fleets? *(JAS)*

One of the problems with a municipal operation is that some ratepayers were accustomed to regard it as a personalised alternative to a taxi service. In October 1953 the Chester Golf Club asked for the Curzon Park service, which was not remunerative as it was, to be extended to near to the entrance to the Club, which would have made it even less likely to make money. This request was not met with any approbation.

The financial position of the undertaking was beginning to worry councillors by this time as the numbers of passengers had started to fall. A loss was made in 1953/4.

On 22 October 1953 it was decided to reduce the service to Huntington, as the number of servicemen at Saighton was falling, and in addition to divert outward only journeys to Eaton Hall via Eccleston Avenue. They continued to return via Eaton Road.

The General Manager thought that it would be sensible to curtail both the Vicar's Cross and the Trooper Inn services, the former at Marbury Road and the latter at Belgrave Road, both within the Ring Road. A wrangle took place about turning points, with the County Council (in the area of which both these points were) suggesting turning at the respective roundabouts on the Ring Road, but the licensing authority was unhappy about the suggestion so far as it related to Vicar's Cross, although there were a few journeys which did terminate there. An earlier query in 1950 had revealed that 2 journeys terminated at the Ring Road, and 74 ran all the way through to the junction with Littleton Lane. However, Astin did take the view that the service from Vicar's Cross to Saltney should be extended along Victoria Road to Green Lane, to serve the new housing there which it had been indicated was a desirable objective. Thus, while the arguing over turning points continued, on 26 April 1954 some journeys to Saltney were extended to Victoria Road, and most of these no longer ran through to the Trooper Inn, but rather stopped short at the corner of Christleton Road and Heath Lane, well within the other turning points which had been put forward.

1954 saw the arrival of no fewer than seven further Guy Arab IVs. They came to Chester throughout the year. The first three, which came in January and February, had four bay bodies, which were unusual at that time, and were built by Guy themselves, but on Park Royal frames and to the

A nearside view of another of the 1954 Guys with Park Royal bodies, 4, with typical half-timbered buildings in the background. *(OS)*

Exposed radiators ended after the Guy bodied Guys and later in 1954 four Massey-bodied Arabs arrived, of which 10 was seen outside the Queen Hotel bound for Saughall. *(OS)*

designs of the latter. The other four had Massey bodies on the traditional lines, that is with five bays. However, the substantial change with all these deliveries is that so called "tin fronts" were fitted instead of the exposed radiators which were found on the rest of the fleet. The concealed radiators on these and later batches were well-designed and added to the dignified look of the fleet.

On 3 January 1955 more journeys to Blacon were introduced, this time from the Town Hall via Saughall Road to Egerton Road corner. From the same date the services to Saughall itself were diverted from St Chad's Road to a more direct and newly-constructed section of Saughall Road, on the outskirts of the estate. The Blacon services still ran via St Chad's Road and the general frequency then was every 20 minutes to Stamford Road and every 20 minutes to Egerton Road, which was just short of the former terminal at Mayfield Road, to which a few extras were still run.

In April 1955, some services on the 4 from Curzon Park were extended from Christleton Church to Christleton Girls' School, like the 3, and off-peak services on the 3 were cut back. The Newtown service (3) was not proving well-used, and this reduction permitted an extra single-decker to be used on the 2, which was being overcrowded.

Once again there was a change in management. The fourth General Manager since 1945 was appointed with effect from 16 May 1955, and he was to prove much more long-lasting. Harold Johnson Hooley (1909-88) finally achieved that which he had wanted for some time. His name is always associated with the Guy Arab era in Chester, but as seen it was, in fact, his predecessor who had re-introduced the marque to the city under peacetime conditions rather than it being forced on the undertaking during the war.

On 28 September 1955 there was more pressure on the Transport Committee to extend services in Blacon along Highfield Road, at the western side of the estate. Hooley advised that the road was too narrow, but the committee had a trial conducted with a single-deck bus and decided that a three-month trial should be instituted. Thus, on 12 December 1955 the somewhat unsatisfactory single-deck service (2) along Blacon Hall Road was extended westwards up Blacon Avenue and then back across the railway line, this time by the Saughall Road bridge over it, and on to Highfield Road, to the junction with Oakfield Road, at the western side of the estate. This resulted in yet more overcrowding on the vehicles, and also to complaints because the short section to Ludlow Road was abandoned.

Another seven Guy Arabs came in to the fleet in 1955. The first two, which arrived in January, were to a similar specification to the four which had arrived at the end of the preceding year. However, the remaining five, which came in September and October, had 5-cylinder engines and seated 58 instead of 56 in their Massey bodies. This was designed to save fuel, and Chester was flat enough for the extra power provided by 6 cylinders not to be required.

The familiar Coach and Horses Hotel is to the right of 17, one of the 1955 delivery of eight Guy Arabs with Massey bodies, loading for Blacon. *(OS)*

The arrival of the new vehicles was balanced to some extent by disposals of those utility vehicles which had not been rebodied. Two of the 1942 Guy Arabs were sold in 1954 and exported to what was than called Salisbury, Southern Rhodesia, for further use. By 1955 only the four last utility Daimlers were still offering their passengers wooden slatted seats: obviously the 1949 resolution to replace these had not been carried through to full effect.

One helpful development in 1955 was that it was agreed by all concerned that Transport House should be demolished completely, and the space realised for the fleet, save that a small new lavatory block for the conductresses should be built.

In 1956 no new vehicles were acquired, a contrast to the past few years, but seven of the eight post-war Daimlers were sent for rebuilding to Samlesbury Engineering, near Blackburn, which was one of the many firms which had turned to the production of bodywork after the war, but later moved more into refurbishment of existing bodies. This further modernised the fleet.

There was one step taken at this time which was extremely retrograde. Hooley obviously did not approve of the conventional timetables which had been being used and he decided to revert with effect from 14 May 1956 to lists of departures, and these continued to be issued throughout his long tenure. There were other oddities in them, not least that the notes always used the outdated spelling form "shewn" instead of "shown", which dated from pre-war timetables. It does not appear that they were cheaper to print, because they still appeared in booklets.

It is fair to say that the Chester timetables of this era are as difficult to understand as any. Even this author, who has had very long experience of interpreting timetables and other publicity material issued by a variety of operators at many dates, has always struggled with these Chester productions, and they were at odds with the generally well-run municipal undertaking. How the average passenger managed to make sense of them is open to conjecture. By this time there were many complications as to departure points, especially in Blacon and in Saltney, and many times had both prefixes and suffixes to indicate where they were coming from and going to.

The highest-numbered of the 1955 deliveries was 18, seen here, unusually, in a suburban setting. *(OS)*

There was a further reorganisation of services with effect from the May 1956 timetable. The Saltney service (6), was linked with Huntington (Rake & Pikel) instead of with Vicar's Cross, and Vicar's Cross was linked to Eccleston Avenue (12). Journeys continued to run also from General Station to Eccleston Avenue (13), and the Eccleston and Eaton Hall service was renumbered 14. Eaton Hall had a better service at this time than earlier, because of the training school.

The 1956 reorganisation also saw the first cutback. The former 11/12 circle to Piper's Ash ceased to operate as such save in the morning peak (although strangely not the evening peak), and services became:

9. General Station-Hoole Lane-Piper's Ash, with a few journeys continuing as a circle;
10. Town Hall-Green Lane-Piper's Ash-Hoole Lane-Town Hall (few journeys);
11. Town Hall-Green Lane.

The effect of this was to end much operation on Green Lane beyond Grove Avenue junction and, of course, take away nearly all of the circular operation, which enabled access from much of east Chester to the City Hospital in Hoole Lane. It is not clear what the rationale was for running the circle in the morning, but not in the evening. It is certainly true that there was pressure at this time to reduce deficits, but Blacon of course remained an exception to the cuts.

On 17 December 1956 there were yet more complications introduced to the Blacon services. Some journeys, still designated as 1, were introduced along the eastern section of St Chad's Road, then via Blacon Point Road and Morton Road to Furne Road, with some running on along Highfield Road to Oakfield Road, at the western side of the estate. The General Manager was very reluctant to continue running along Highfield Road, but was pressed to do so by the committee; this only involved about five journeys a day, but it enabled the unsatisfactory extension of the 2 to be cut back to the corner of Blacon Avenue and Lichfield Road, but it was diverted via Malvern Road so that it again served Ludlow Road en route. These alterations left a considerable portion of Blacon Avenue unserved, an unsatisfactory result, but this was a continuing consequence of the inability to access Blacon from the Parkgate Road.

On 23 July 1956 it was decided that the services to Egerton and Stamford Road should be diverted from St Chad's Road on to Saughall Road, as had been the through services to Saughall. The new Furne Road/Oakfield Road service continued to run along the southern portion of the doglegged St Chad's Road.

Hooley thought that the Curzon Park leg of the Christleton service should be abandoned and instead those journeys running through to Saltney

The Cliveden Road stance has on it 19, one of the 1957 Guy Arabs with 60-seat Massey bodies, which were then the largest capacity vehicles in the fleet. *(OS)*

(Victoria Road) should run through Curzon Park and down Mount Pleasant, which was, of course, an old idea. However, it was not reintroduced and the existing position continued.

There were no new service developments in 1957, unusually, although the first part of the year saw a reduction in services because of the fuel situation after the Suez Crisis. However, the year did see the arrival of five new Guy Arabs, between March and May. They had similar tin fronts to the 1955 arrivals, and also had 5-cylinder engines. Their Massey bodies seated 60, making them the largest-capacity vehicles in the fleet. This year also saw the replacement of "Chester Corporation" as the fleetname carried on the buses by "City of Chester". It was also in January 1957 that work

In 1959 Chester acquired two 1946 Guy Arabs with Park Royal bodies to replace the Davies-bodied Fodens. 56 is seen at the Station bound for Saughall.

Number 56 was parked near to the Football Stadium waiting for the end of the match. *(OS)*

finally began on construction of the much-delayed garage extension. It was carried out in two phases and the second was completed in 1958.

By the end of 1957, the fleet had been comprehensively updated. The only wartime vehicles still in the fleet were the four rebodied Guy Arabs, and one remaining utility Daimler, 59, which remained in service until 1961, when it was sold after 16 years' running, a long time for a wartime vehicle which had not been rebodied. In fact, after 1957 no new vehicles were taken into stock until 1961.

1958 was a quiet year for service development also. On 28 July another new one-way scheme, involving Frodsham Street, caused the diversion of service 9 journeys to the Town Hall instead of the Station. This also meant that all services to the Station save the 3, which continued to serve St Anne Street, now ran up City Road. There was an increase in frequency to Saltney (Ring Road) so that journeys ran every 30 minutes: this reflected the increased housing development in the area.

The Great Boughton area, to the east of the city, was developing fast by this time and a new Secondary Modern (later High) School was opened at Christleton, to cater for the increased demand. Journeys on the Vicar's Cross service were extended through Littleton to the new school, although only twice a day at appropriate times, with effect from 1 September 1958. The following year some journeys were also extended from Green Lane via Piper's Ash, Hare Lane and Littleton, also to the school. It was also suggested at this time, but not implemented, that all Christleton Village services should run on from Vicar's Cross via Littleton, which would have avoided the problematic canal bridge and greatly

enhanced the service to Littleton. At that point, only the last bus to Vicar's Cross was so extended.

Eaton Hall cadet school was being run down in numbers at this time and consequentially the service there and to Eccleston was reduced in September 1958.

On 6 October 1958 the two Davies-bodied Fodens, 79 and 80, were stripped down, in consequence of rot being discovered in them. Samlesbury said that they could not repair them, and Massey said new bodies would cost £1,950 each. It was decided that rebodying them was not economic and they were withdrawn. This was a result of inadequacies in the original bodies and was not attributable to any mechanical deficiencies; the remaining Fodens in the fleet were giving good service and continued to do so for many years thereafter.

The solution adopted was the purchase of two second-hand vehicles, the first ever owned. These arrived in February 1959 and were Guy Arabs with exposed radiators, 6-cylinder engines and Park Royal bodies, which had been new to Southampton Corporation in 1946, and were thus five years older than the Fodens. They cost only £450 each. Southampton used Guys extensively, and the buses were rebuilt by Chester to provide their standard indicator displays. The Arabs fitted in well with the fleet, and were retained for some years. No new vehicles were, of course, purchased this year.

After a period in which the central portion of Blacon Avenue had been left unserved, from 11 June 1959 some of the services to Stamford Road were extended to Ludlow Road: this meant a roundabout trip, but was the best that could be managed; this was initially an experiment, but was continued thereafter.

7: BUS OPERATION 1960-74

No new vehicles arrived in 1960: however, the route network was further complicated. This was reflected in the way in which the timetables were displayed and a new booklet dated 17 October 1960 demonstrated this very clearly.

The lists of departures worked perfectly well with, for example, the 7/8 Cliveden Road circle, which normally had no variations and was in any event a frequent service. They were, however, virtually impossible to understand when, for example, dealing with services from Saltney: by this time there were buses from Ring Road, Victoria Road/Green Lane junction, West View and a few journeys from Irving's Crescent, which was part of the way down Victoria Road; these had been suggested in 1957 but it is not clear when they were introduced. Thus, the list of services from Saltney has prefix signs to show if they came from Ring Road, Victoria Road or Irving's Crescent, or no prefix if they came from West View; each then has a suffix to show where they were going: T to the Trooper Inn, H to Huntingdon Shops, R to Rake & Pikel and odd journeys S to General Station.

The Blacon service was even more difficult to comprehend. Most services from General Station ran through to Saughall, but some went to various parts of Blacon. From the Town Hall all journeys to Egerton Road, Stamford Road, Furne Road, Oakfield Road and Blacon Camp were numbered 1, as were the extended services to Ludlow Road via Blacon Avenue. A simple sketch map would have assisted a great deal.

Another complication was caused by extending nearly all evening and Sunday journeys on 12 (Vicar's Cross) to Littleton and Christleton, so that the 3 and 4 could cease operating at those times: this meant that Littleton had a disproportionately good service in the evenings, because Christleton was reached from Vicar's Cross at these times by running through it. It was requested that some journeys running to the Trooper Inn should cover the Heath Lane section, left unserved when the 3 and 4 were not running, but that was not done.

In 1960 King's School, the leading independent boys' school in the area, moved from the city centre to new premises in Wrexham Road, outside the urban area. The frosty but reasonably cooperative relationship between the Council and Crosville meant they mutually agreed to divide up the new traffic. Chester ran two buses to and from the school from the General Station, and Crosville two from Northgate Station. Each railway station was very near their respective garages. The Chester service was nominally given the number 15 but was usually shown on the Eccleston Avenue chart.

No new vehicles had arrived since 1957, but the winds of change were beginning to affect even this bastion of conservatism. On 13 February 1960 Daimler offered to demonstrate a Fleetline en route to Belfast. However, the taking into service of rear-engined vehicles was a step too far for Chester at this time.

On 7 March 1960 the committee said that they needed new buses of either 27 feet or 30 feet length, but wanted a demonstration of the larger size. This was soon arranged: on 15 March 1960 Wolverhampton sent one of their 30 feet long Guys to be trialled in the difficult, traffic-congested, narrow, streets of Chester. That was a much more predictable way for the city to move forward than buying Fleetlines or Leyland Atlanteans. It was then decided that larger buses should indeed be ordered and four tenders were received: predictably, that from Guy was accepted. Three quotations were requested for bodywork, but only Massey responded.

It was thus with customary caution that Chester moved forward. In June and July 1961 three Guy Arab IVs with Massey bodies arrived, and June of the following year saw the arrival of another four. All seven were eight feet wide, 30 feet long, and fitted with air brakes, as well as with 73-seat bodies with front entrances and sliding doors. Thus, they were much larger than any other vehicles ever owned by Chester. All these vehicles were fitted with the so-called Johannesburg fronts, a relatively unusual form of grille, so named because it had originally been supplied to South Africa, and they also had 6-cylinder engines, no doubt required because of their size and weight.

On 10 July 1961, or just as these first larger vehicles were arriving, the Council resolved to purchase another four for 1963/4 and also a new single-decker, which they required to be demonstrated on the Christleton route; the effect

would have been to increase the size of the fleet, because of the continuing need for more journeys to Blacon. No new single-deckers had been bought since shortly after the end of the war, so that was a possible new departure, but in fact it was not taken forward for some considerable time.

Guys were by this time in financial difficulties, largely attributable to its South African subsidiary, and on 9 October 1961 it was reported to Chester that the company was in the hands of receivers and that the warranties on the recently delivered vehicles would be repudiated. This unwelcome news did not endure for long, because the Jaguar organisation took over Guy, and the guarantees were reinstated.

The arrival of the 1961 Guys permitted the withdrawal of the last Daimler utility bus and of the two Guys which had been rebodied by DJ Davies. The bodies which had been fitted had been much more successful than those provided for the two Fodens, but these two were ready for withdrawal well before those vehicles rebodied by Massey.

The arrival of these three Guy Arabs in 1961 marked a revolution in transport in Chester as they were thirty feet long, eight feet wide, carried 73 and had front entrances with Johannesburg grills. 25 is at the Town Hall on the Blacon circle via Parkgate Road. *(OS)*

The door arrangements of the 1961 Arabs are very clear on this nearside view of 26 at the Town Hall waiting to leave for Piper's Ash. *(OS)*

In 1962 a further four similar vehicles arrived; 28 is seen in the city centre with characteristic Chester architecture behind it, as it travels to Saltney. *(OS)*

On 4 December 1961 the unsatisfactory single-deck service 2 was finally withdrawn, and was replaced by extra double-decker journeys along Blacon Avenue from Saughall Road, or in other words from the west end of the estate. The real problem was that there was then no access to Blacon from the east other than under the low bridge, but by taking this course at least the passengers could be carried. There had been yet more complaints shortly before that of people being unable to get on to the small capacity single-deckers and having to wait.

On 12 February 1962 amendments to the gyratory system at the Liverpool Road/Parkgate Road confluence meant that all the Blacon services were diverted via Walpole Street instead of Chichester Street. In later years both streets were used, Walpole Street outward and Chichester Street inward.

On 28 May 1962 the Vicar's Cross service 12 was extended about 200 yards into Littleton Lane itself. It is a mark of the way in which Transport Committees conducted their business that the precise location of the terminal stop there occupied the business of the body for very much longer than did the expenditure of considerable sums on new vehicles. The change was brought about at the request of the Cheshire police, who were worried by the terminus being on the main road. Then on 12 June 1962 the recurring issue of the headgear for conductresses again required much discussion. It was resolved that they should be provided with air hostess style hats and if they wore anything on their heads, it should be these.

On 18 June 1962 the Oakfield Road journeys in Blacon were extended about 100 yards to Longdale Drive. However, as late as 1965 the timetable was telling prospective passengers that a service to Longdale Drive would carry Oakfield Road on its destination blinds, to add yet more uncertainty in the minds of those wanting to get home or visit relatives.

On 3 December 1962 it was resolved that a further four Guys be purchased and, on this occasion, no alternative tenders were requested. It was also decided that a second-hand single-decker should be purchased from Nottingham. At £425 this was a much cheaper option than buying a new bus but gave no encouragement to the use of one-man operation. The small single-decker fleet consisted throughout the 1950s only of the four Regals of 1946/7. One was withdrawn in 1962 and another in 1963. The purchase from Nottingham in January 1963 was of a second-hand AEC Regal with a 35-seat rear-entrance East Lancs body, which had been new in June 1951, at which time many operators were in any event turning to underfloor-engined single-deckers. In the event, this was to be the last half cab single-decker in the Chester fleet.

After the Nottingham vehicle had arrived, it was resolved that one of the existing Regals, 68 (HFM 176) should be converted to a towing vehicle but this was not in the event done. It is clear that the 1946/7 Regals were coming to the end of their life by this time.

Consideration was then given to reinstating the Piper's Ash circle, but it was thought that

In 1963 Chester, instead of buying a new single-decker, bought a second-hand AEC Regal from Nottingham, which it retained until 1970. 51 is seen in Bridge Street. *(TL/RM)*

crossing the Ring Road twice was difficult and no action was taken: it was also thought that further developments should await new building projected in the area.

The four Guy Arabs with Massey bodies which had been ordered were delivered in November 1963, although this time they were Arab Vs rather than IVs. They too had 73-seat front-entrance bodies, but they differed in appearance considerably from the previous two years' deliveries, because they reverted to the use of a conventional tin front grille rather than the Johannesburg front, which had enjoyed only a short period as an option and was never popular.

Late 1963 finally saw a development which had been needed for many years and should have been done before the extensive building had taken place at Blacon. Blacon Avenue was extended eastwards, via a new bridge over the Shropshire Union Canal, so that it met Parkgate Road, which, of course, the Corporation had ceased operating along after the 1932 agreement with Crosville. This new bridge meant that Chester could run into Blacon from the other side from Saughall Road.

However, the only way was along Parkgate Road. That had very small local traffic on the intermediate section, but Crosville was anxious to

The 1963 Arabs were of Mark V but also had Massey front-entrance bodies: however, they reverted to the use of tin fronts. 31 is at the Town Hall loading for the Blacon circle via Saughall Road. *(OS)*

retain it. It is a measure of the way in which the 1932 agreement still affected local transport, and the passive attitude of the Traffic Commissioners, that initially Chester only got permission to run into Blacon Avenue via Parkgate Road subject to conditions that on outward journeys no passenger could be set down between Mason Street (by the junction of Liverpool and Parkgate Roads) and the Bishops' School on Blacon Avenue; conversely passengers could not be picked up between the School and Delamere Street. This embargo made the new service much less successful than would otherwise have been the case. The number 2 was revived for these journeys, and they ran to Ludlow Road and then along Blacon Avenue to serve Lichfield Road and Stamford Road, approximately hourly. This began on 2 December 1963.

It is somewhat ironic that on 7 September 1964 a petition was presented to the Council requesting that the single-deck service via Blacon Hall Road should be restored. Needless to say, no action was taken on this.

The 1965 timetable for the 3 and 4, with a multitude of notes: how to make a simple timetable incomprehensible.

Right: Another page from the 1965 timetable, making the Saltney service much more difficult to understand than it should have been.

Route 3—General Rly. Stn. to Town Hall, via St. Anne Street —Christleton (Girls' School)

Route 4—Earlsway (Curzon Park)-Westminster Bank–Christleton and Littleton via Stocks Lane.

MONDAY to SATURDAY

HOUR	To Christleton and/or Littleton from				To Earlsway from:			Town H. to Gn. Sn.	HOUR
	Gn. Sn.	Town Hall	Earls-way	W'ster Bank	Chris'n. G. Sch.	Little-ton	Browns		
A.M.	mins past hour								A.M.
7-	—	—	—	43	—	—	—	—	7
8-	0	10, NS23P	30LG	43L / 43L	0, 30T / †36NST	—	13H	—	8
9-	5T	—	30LG	—	—	0*M	13G	—	9
10-	NS35T	—	30H	43	—	0	13G	—	10
11-	—	—	30H	43	0	—	13H	NS50B	11
12-	5	10	30H	43	0, 30S	—	13H	50	12
P.M.									P.M.
1-	—	—	30H	43	0	—	13H	—	1
2-	NS15T, 5TSO	—	30H	43	0*	—	13H	—	2
3-	5	10	30LG	43L	0, 30S	—	13H	50	3
4-	5	10	30G	43	30S	0	13H	50	4
5-	5	10	30LG	43L	0, 30S	—	13H	50	5
6-	5	10, †37	30SH	43D	30S, 53C	0	13G	50	6
7-	—	†7, †37	—	—	23C, 53C	—	—	—	7
8-	—	†37	—	—	53C	—	—	—	8
9-	—	†7SO †37	—	—	23CSO, 53C	—	—	—	9
10-	—	†7, †40	—	—	23C, 56CG	—	—	—	10

SUNDAY

p.m.

Town Hall to Christleton: †2-20, †2-55, †4-05, †4-40, †5-50, †7-00, †8-10, †9-20, †9-55, †10-30

Christleton (Girls' School) to Town Hall: †2-37T, †3-12T, †4-22T, †4-57T, †6-07T, †7-17T, †8-27T, †9-37T, †10-12T, †10-47CG

B—From Blacon Shelter

C—To Eccleston Avenue via Vicars Cross and the City.

CG—To General Station via Vicars Cross and City Road.

D—To General Station via City Road   G—Via Grosvenor Road.

H—Via Handbridge.   L—To Littleton via Christleton.

NS—Not Saturday.   P—Via Pipers Ash, Hare Lane and Vicars Cross.

S—To Gen. Station via Town Hall.   T—To Town Hall only.

SH—To General Station via Handbridge and City Road.

SO—Saturdays only.   †—Via Vicars Cross

* Direct via Christleton Road, NOT via Heath Lane, Monday to Saturday.

*M—Direct via Christleton Road, NOT via Heath Lane, Monday to Friday.

9

Route 3—General Rly. Stn. to Town Hall, via St. Anne Street —Christleton (Girls' School)

Route 4—Earlsway (Curzon Park)-Westminster Bank–Christleton and Littleton via Stocks Lane.

MONDAY to SATURDAY

HOUR	To Christleton and/or Littleton from				To Earlsway from:			Town H. to Gn. Sn.	HOUR
	Gn. Sn.	Town Hall	Earls-way	W'ster Bank	Chris'n. G. Sch.	Little-ton	Browns		
A.M.	mins past hour								A.M.
7-	—	—	—	43	—	—	—	—	7
8-	0	10, NS23P	30LG	43L / 43L	0, 30T / †36NST	—	13H	—	8
9-	5T	—	30LG	—	—	0*M	13G	—	9
10-	NS35T	—	30H	43	—	0	13G	—	10
11-	—	—	30H	43	0	—	13H	NS50B	11
12-	5	10	30H	43	0, 30S	—	13H	50	12
P.M.									P.M.
1-	—	—	30H	43	0	—	13H	—	1
2-	NS15T, 5TSO	—	30H	43	0*	—	13H	—	2
3-	5	10	30LG	43L	0, 30S	—	13H	50	3
4-	5	10	30G	43	30S	0	13H	50	4
5-	5	10	30LG	43L	0, 30S	—	13H	50	5
6-	5	10, †37	30SH	43D	30S, 53C	0	13G	50	6
7-	—	†7, †37	—	—	23C, 53C	—	—	—	7
8-	—	†37	—	—	53C	—	—	—	8
9-	—	†7SO †37	—	—	23CSO, 53C	—	—	—	9
10-	—	†7, †40	—	—	23C, 56CG	—	—	—	10

SUNDAY

p.m.

Town Hall to Christleton: †2-20, †2-55, †4-05, †4-40, †5-50, †7-00, †8-10, †9-20, †9-55, †10-30

Christleton (Girls' School) to Town Hall: †2-37T, †3-12T, †4-22T, †4-57T, †6-07T, †7-17T, †8-27T, †9-37T, †10-12T, †10-47CG

B—From Blacon Shelter

C—To Eccleston Avenue via Vicars Cross and the City.

CG—To General Station via Vicars Cross and City Road.

D—To General Station via City Road   G—Via Grosvenor Road.

H—Via Handbridge.   L—To Littleton via Christleton.

NS—Not Saturday.   P—Via Pipers Ash, Hare Lane and Vicars Cross.

S—To Gen. Station via Town Hall.   T—To Town Hall only.

SH—To General Station via Handbridge and City Road.

SO—Saturdays only.   †—Via Vicars Cross

* Direct via Christleton Road, NOT via Heath Lane, Monday to Saturday.

*M—Direct via Christleton Road, NOT via Heath Lane, Monday to Friday.

9

Route 5—Saltney Ring Rd., West View and/or Victoria Rd. to Trooper Inn

Route 6— do. do. do. do. to Rake and Pikel

MONDAY—FRIDAY	SATURDAY	SUNDAY
A.M. mins. past HOUR:	A.M. minutes past HOUR:	A.M. minutes past HOUR:
6–0T, (via Cliveden Shops & G. Stn) (*20T, 35R, via Gen. Stn.), 50T.	6–0T, (via C'den Shops & Gen. Stn.) (*20T, 35R, via Gen. Stn.), 50T.	6–20s, via C'den Shops
7–*2R, †10T, 20R, *25T, 40T, †50T.	7–*2R, †10T, 20R, *30T, 40T, †50T.	7–0B, via C'den Shops and City Hosp.
8–*0R, §10T, ‡15R, 20T *30R 40T, §42C, †45T, 50R.	8–*0R, §10T, 20T, *30R, 40T, †45T. 50R.	8–*0R, via C'den Shops and Gen. Stn.
9–*0T, 10R, 20T, †20s, 30H *40T, 50R.	9–*0T, 10R, 20T, †30R, *40T, *50R.	9–0s, via C'den Shops
10–0T, *10H, 20T, §30R, *40T, 50H.	10–*0T, *10R, *20T, *30R, †30s, *40T, 50R.	10–†15T, *45T.
11–0T, *10R, 20T, †30H, *40T, 50R.	11–0T, *10R, 20T, 30R, *40T, †50R.	11–0R, 15T, *30R, 45T.
12–0T, *10R, 20T, §30R, *40T, 50H.	12–0T, *10R, 20T, 30R, *40T, 50R, †55H.	12–5R, †15T, *30R, 45T.
P.M.	P.M.	P.M.
1–0T, *10R, 20T, §30R, *40T, 50R.	1–0T, *10R, 20T, 30R, *40T, 50R.	1–0R, 20T, *40T.
2–0T, *10H, 20T, †30R, 40T, 50H.	2–†0T, *10R, 20T, 30R, *40T, 50R.	2–†0T, *10R, 20T, 30R, *40T, 50R.
3–0T, *10R, 20T, §30H, *40T, 50R.	3–0T, †5H, *10R, 20T, 30R, *40T, 50R.	3–§0T, *10R, 20T, 30R, *40T, 50R.
4–0T, 10R, *20T, 30R, †32B, *40T. 50R.	4–†0T, 10R, *20T, 30R, *40T, 50R.	4–§0T, 10R, *20T, 30R, *40T, 50R.
5–0T, *10R. 20T. 30R. †32T, 35s, *40T, 50R, 55R.	5–0T, *10R, †15B, 20T, 30R, *40T. 50R.	5–§0T, *10R, 20T, 30R *40T, 50R.
6–0T, *10R, *20T, §20s, 30R, †32s. *40T, 50R.	6–0T, *10R, †20T, 30R, *40T, 50R.	6–†0T, *10R, 20T, 30R, *40T, 50R.
7–*0T, *10R, †20T, 30R, *40T, 50R.	7–0T, *10R, †20T, 30R, *40T, 50R	7–§0T, *10R, 20T, 30R, *40T. 50R.
8–0T, 10R, *20T, 30R, †40T, 50R.	8–0T, 10R, *20T, 30R, †40T, 50R.	8–†0T, 10R, *20T, 30R, 40T, 50R.
9–*0T, 10R, 20T, 30R, *40T, 50R.	9–*0T, 10R, 20T, 30R, *40T, 50R.	9–§0T, *10R, 20T, 30R, *40T, 50R.
10–†0T, 10H *20T, 30R 40T, †50s.	10–†0T, 10R, *20T, 30R, 40T, 45R, †50s	10–§0T, 10R, *20T, 30R, 40T, †50s.
11–*0s, 10s, 20s.	11–*0s, 10s, 20s.	11–*0s, 10s, 20s.

B–To Heath Lane   *–From Ring Road.   C–To Town Hall

s–To Gen. Rly. Stn.   ‡–From Anchor Hotel.   §–From Irvings

†–From Victoria Rd.   H–To Huntington Shops only   Crescent only.

T–To Trooper Inn.   R–To Rake and Pikel.

From the same date that the new service began, the Blacon Camp journeys were discontinued, as that area was being redeveloped for housing. Yet another variant of the 1 was introduced to replace these, running along Blacon Point Road to what was described as a temporary terminus at Treborth Road. That part of the estate was being rapidly developed at this time.

The very restrictive conditions attached to the Parkgate Road service were in due course relaxed, so that Chester could pick up and set down along it: however, this did not take place until June 1967. Thus, the ratepayers were relieved from seeing their own corporation buses sailing past them, unable to carry them into town. It is, however, a measure of the way in which the licensing system worked that Chester only obtained that concession by allowing Crosville to extend their Sealand Road route from Blacon Point, near the estate, to Treborth Road, within it, and also permitted them to pick up for Christleton and Saughall. It is also noteworthy that amidst all the many notes in the timetables of the time, there was not one explaining the restrictions. The Crosville service C55 from Blacon ran only hourly, so was no great rival to the Corporation services.

There was another positive move at this time. With effect from 20 January 1964 the 11, which had been cut back to Grove Avenue in 1956, was re-extended a short distance along Green Lane to terminate at the junction with Queen's Road.

Another development at this time was the consideration of the diversion of a few Eccleston Avenue journeys into the Queen's Park area, via Queen's Park Road, Victoria Crescent, St George's Crescent and Meadows Lane. This minor matter was first raised on 9 March 1964, but then required alteration of some corners on the route. It was announced as beginning operating in August 1965, although even then only on two journeys in any direction, but it does not appear to have actually started until January 1966.

On 9 October 1964 the Transport Committee was asked to introduce the 24-hour clock. This innovatory gesture was firmly rejected. A year or so later, on 9 October 1965 Hooley was asked to report on different types of timetables, a reform which was badly needed; however, characteristically, it was resolved that no action be taken.

Chester remained firmly devoted to the Guy Arab for its double-deckers, a predilection which

The 1965 delivery of Guy Arab Vs with Massey bodies is exemplified by 35, as it breaches the City Wall en route for Saltney. *(TL/RM)*

by this time was looking unfashionable. It was also looking entirely predictable: on 9 October 1964 Guy and Massey were asked to extend their previous tenders, rather than asking for competitive quotes.

Thus, in July and August 1965 a further four Arab Vs arrived, the first in the fleet with suffix letter registration marks. They too had 73-seat Massey bodies and, as with the others, were to prove reliable and long-lasting. On 15 September 1965 it was agreed that a further three be bought, and this time six firms were asked to tender for the bodywork, but only Massey did so.

The continued expansion of the southern area of the Blacon estate involved Blacon Point Road and Western Avenue being extended so that they met each other. This meant that the services to Treborth Road and to Furne Road via Blacon Point Road could be joined as a circular. This was done with effect from the timetable of 28 June 1965 and the service ran anti-clockwise, via Blacon Point Road, Morton Road, Furne Road, Western Avenue and back on to Blacon Point Road, or clockwise, the other way around. The timetable showing these changes was characteristically difficult to follow. The service ran about every 20 minutes, and thus every 40 minutes in each direction around the loop. With effect from the same day, the 2 was re-extended to Highfield Road, terminating at Longdale Road, replacing the service there via Blacon Point Road. The overcrowding issue had, of course, disappeared once double-deckers could be used and there was no need to use the road under the low bridge.

The regular service from the city to Saughall Road had, of course, ceased operating many years before, but a traffic notice indicated that with effect from 22 September 1966 an untimetabled duplicate which had run every weekday at 8.45am from the corner of Saughall Road and Whipcord Lane would cease operating: it was a relic of the early years of the undertaking's bus services.

1966 saw the arrival of another three Arab Vs with the customary Massey bodies in September. However, a more revolutionary new vehicle in August of that year had been a Leyland Tiger Cub with Massey 40-seat body fitted with two doors: the centre door was used for exits. This was the first underfloor-engined single-decker purchased, 15 years after they became very common: it also afforded the possibility of one-man operation, which none of the other buses in the fleet did, but was not initially so used.

On 18 May 1967 the Sunday service to Eccleston and Eaton Hall (which would have been a prime candidate for one-man buses) was cut back to the village, at the request of the management of the Hall.

On 3 July 1967 Great Boughton Parish Council asked for the extension of the Piper's Ash service across the Ring Road, so that it again served the village, from which it had been cut back many years earlier. This approach was rebuffed, but

Chester finally began purchasing new single-deckers in 1966 and took a Leyland Leopard with Massey dual door body in that and the two succeeding years. This is the 1967 addition, 53, on its way to Curzon Park. (TL/RM)

it was followed by a long-running debate over the turning point for the 9 service on that route. The initial suggestion was that buses ran round Cedar Drive, Alder Grove and Piper's Lane, thus enabling a reversal to be avoided. Following representations, it was then decided on 30 October 1967 that buses should run off the main road into Piper's Lane and reverse into Alder Grove, thus avoiding such a manoeuvre on Hoole Lane. A local resident then complained and it was decided to investigate the purchase of part of the car park of the Piper's Hotel to form a turning point. The brewery agreed to sell some land for £200 and in 1968 resolution was thus eventually reached.

On 11 September 1967 the long-established Saughall service was extended further through the village to terminate at Saughall Hey: Crosville were asked in advance to agree to this and did.

In September 1967 another Leyland Tiger Cub was delivered, to similar specification as that which had arrived the year before. A third arrived in December 1968, which turned out to have the last body completed wholly by Massey. These three new single-deckers meant that the two Regals new to Chester could be withdrawn, after long service. The former Nottingham Regal remained in service until 1970, by which time it was itself almost 20 years old. Leyland do not appear to have been interested at this time in Chester's double-decker requirements and only tendered for the single-deckers.

On 4 March 1968 Chester was again asked to use the 24-hour clock: again, there was an abrupt refusal.

On 22 July 1968 a nettle was finally grasped after the problem had been ignored for so long. This was the introduction of a comprehensive system of route suffixes for all the variants in Blacon.

The underlying principle was retained that services into the estate via Saughall Road were given number 1 plus a letter, and those via Parkgate Road number 2 plus a letter.

The two circles introduced in 1965 were given the numbers 1A (anti-clockwise) and 1B (clockwise). The Saughall service from the Station was numbered 1D. Services to Egerton Road, which were in effect short workings of that, were numbered 1E. Services via Saughall Road, returning via Blacon Avenue and Parkgate Road, were numbered 1F in that direction and 2F in the other. Those running to Blacon Avenue (Lichfield Road) via Saughall Road in both directions, which

51 is outside Brown's, apparently out of service. *(OS)*

were thus short workings of the 1F/2F circle, were numbered 1G. The basic service 2, which had run via Parkgate Road and Blacon Avenue to Longdale Drive, was given the number 2C and became a unidirectional circle through the western part of the estate, running via Highfield Road, Oakfield Road, Auckland Road and Western Avenue, then back on to Blacon Avenue and to town via Parkgate Road. The Manager was firmly against running buses in both directions along the narrow Highfield Road and this was a solution to that problem. The new arrangements gave a much better coverage of the estate, including the Auckland Road area which had been built on the site of the Camp, but meant that the very short section to Longdale Drive was abandoned.

The underlying aspect of all these changes was an attempt to see how circular services could serve the area.

The 1968 system was complicated, but it remained in place for a few years.

In the meantime, Chester continued along its own path of purchasing double-deckers. In March 1967 Massey were taken over by Northern Counties, another Wigan-based bodybuilder. Initially production continued at Massey's Pemberton works and as already set out the last of Chester's three Leyland Leopards was the last vehicle completed wholly there.

In March 1969 three more Guy Arabs arrived and a further three came in October. The bodies were all ordered from Massey but the work was largely carried out by Northern Counties. Both batches had Massey style lower decks, but Northern Counties style upper decks: all seated 73. They were very traditional and perhaps rather stately, but good looking and well finished vehicles.

In 1969 Chester Corporation took delivery of six forward-entrance Guy Arab V double-deckers with Massey style lower saloons and NCME style upper saloons following the takeover by the latter company. Number 42, shown here, is now preserved. *(JAS)*

The delivery of the second batch of three vehicles, in October 1969, was particularly significant. By this time rear-engined double-deckers were sweeping all before them across the country. These were the last Guy Arabs built and also the last Guy buses built for service in the United Kingdom. It was fitting that they went to Chester, because their arrival meant that the double-deck fleet of 47 was comprised entirely of Guy Arabs, albeit in several variants. The fleet had remained at about 50 since the Second World War, and was exactly such at this time, with the three Tiger Cubs making up the balance.

In the long term, however, there were clouds ahead, as costs were escalating and none of the double-deckers in service could be used for one-man operation. In addition, a careful regime of maintenance meant that the more elderly vehicles had run for many years and would need replacement in the near future.

The minutes are less fulsome in this period: the committee dealing with the buses was that for Public Services and Recreation, which had many other responsibilities and devoted less time to the Transport Undertaking. Relations with Crosville, which had been so difficult for so many years, finally showed some signs of thawing. It was agreed, for example, that on the closure of Northgate Station in 1969 Crosville should run their buses to King's School from the General Station, as did Chester. On 9 June 1969 it was agreed that the two organisations would offer reciprocal free travel to employees going to and from work when in uniform.

The highest numbered of the 47 Guy Arabs, which in 1969 comprised the entire Chester double-deck fleet, was 47, shown in the revised livery inward bound from Cliveden Road. *(OS)*

There was further talk of a full coordination agreement between Chester and Crosville in 1969/70; Crosville was suggesting joint depots and joint use of the new bus station which they wanted to construct in Delamere Street, in place of the on-street stances which had been there for many years. In 1971 the National Bus Company, of which Crosville was by then a part, made an informal approach to purchase the entire Chester undertaking, but this received a very frosty reaction, with Hooley telling the committee that the NBC was practically bankrupt. Then, when the new bus station was opened, Hooley said that Chester would not extend its services there from the Town Hall because it would disrupt the schedules and was in any event unnecessary. Certainly, the Town Hall was much nearer the shopping centre. The real need, which was not addressed, was an interchange point between all local and interurban services at some convenient point.

One of the fascinating questions, to which there is no clear answer, is whether Chester would have wanted to continue to order Guy Arabs had they been available. The major problem in their way would have been the substantial grants becoming available for the purchase of vehicles suitable for one man operation.

Whatever would have happened, in the circumstances in which the Corporation found itself it had to consider its future policy. The decision was taken to order three Daimler Fleetlines with well-tried Gardner engines. They arrived in December 1970, were fitted with Northern Counties bodies of intermediate height and originally seated 74. Northern Counties was the only company with the capacity to tender for the bodies. It was clear that, after a long delay, one man operation of both single- and double-deckers was needed, to avoid financial disaster and this was introduced following long negotiations with the unions.

On 18 January 1971 the evening service to Blacon was revised and more suffixes introduced. A logical circular was introduced, clockwise as 1J, from the Town Hall via Saughall Road, Blacon Point Road, Western Avenue, Blacon Avenue and Parkgate Road back to the Town Hall. The anti-clockwise journeys were numbered 2K. These routes gave good coverage to the estate as a whole and provided a number of links, but at that stage they only applied in the evenings and to occasional other journeys.

50 was one of the first three Daimler Fleetlines, which came in 1970. The giant route number is well shown in this picture on service 6 to Huntington. *(OS)*

At the same time there was another break from the past. Journeys to Eaton Hall had been very popular when the military were using it but had gradually lost traffic. The regular services beyond Eccleston were discontinued and the position reverted to that which had originally prevailed; in other words, an occasional service licence was retained for special events only.

Services run in 1972 were thus as follows, with weekday frequencies:

1A/1B. Town Hall-Saughall Road-Blacon (Rhuddlan Road), 1A out via Furne Road, 1B out via Blacon Point Road) (every 30 minutes on each service).

1D. General Station-Town Hall-Saughall Road-Blacon-Saughall (Saughall Hey) (30 minutes).

1E/2E. Town Hall-Saughall Road (1E) or Parkgate Road (2E)-Blacon (Egerton Road) (extras only).

1F/2F. Town Hall-Saughall Road-Blacon (Stamford Road)-Parkgate Road-Town Hall, 1F out via Saughall Road, 2F out via Parkgate Road (extras only).

1G. Town Hall-Saughall Road-Blacon (Stamford and Lichfield Roads) (extras only).

1H/2H. Extras to Blacon via Saughall Road (1H) or Parkgate Road (2H).

1J. Town Hall-Saughall Road-Blacon (Rhuddlan, Stamford and Lichfield Roads)-Parkgate Road-Town Hall. Unidirectional (see 2K); generally, evenings and Sundays only.

2C. Town Hall-Parkgate Road-Blacon (Lichfield, Stamford and Auckland Roads)-Parkgate Road-Town Hall (every 30 minutes, unidirectional).

2K. Town Hall-Parkgate Road-Blacon (Lichfield, Stamford, Auckland and Rhuddlan Roads)-Saughall Road-Town Hall. Unidirectional (see 1J); generally evenings and Sundays only.

3. General Station-Town Hall-Stocks Lane-Christleton (Girls School) (hourly, not evenings).

4. Curzon Park-City-Stocks Lane-Christleton (hourly, with a few extensions to Littleton).

5. Saltney (Ring Road, with a few journeys from Irving's Crescent or Victoria Road)-City-Trooper Inn (every 20 minutes).

6. Saltney (Ring Road, with a few journeys from Irving's Crescent or Victoria Road)-City-Huntington (Rake & Pikel) (every 20 minutes).

7. Town Hall-Cliveden Estate circular via Hough Green (every 20 minutes).

8. Town Hall-Cliveden Estate circular via Lache Lane (every 20 minutes).

9. Town Hall-Piper's Ash (every 30 minutes).

10. Town Hall-Piper's Ash-Green Lane-Town Hall (occasional).

11. Town Hall- Green Lane (every 30 minutes).

12. Town Hall-Vicar's Cross (every 30 minutes), with some evening and Sunday journeys to Littleton and Christleton Village, and some Sunday journeys running through from Eccleston Avenue.

13. General Station-City-Handbridge (Eccleston Avenue) (every 30 minutes).

14. General Station-City-Handbridge (Eccleston Avenue)-Eccleston Village (seven journeys a day).

This timetable shows that some services were being eroded as traffic fell, particularly those to more affluent areas. Thus Eccleston Avenue had in the heady immediate post-war years a bus every 15 minutes; by 1972 this had been reduced to half-hourly and the service had been integrated with the Eccleston Village buses, which by then all ran via Eccleston Avenue rather than the main road. A very few journeys also ran via the Queen's Park area and there were school day extras to the King's School on Wrexham Road.

Traffic congestion continued to be a real problem in the city, which combined a small and constrained central area with many tourists and also with providing shopping and other services to a wide area of Cheshire and of North Wales. The situation had been alleviated somewhat by the Inner Ring Road, which continued throughout the 1960s and was finally completed in 1972, albeit at the cost of much destruction of property and, incidentally, of diversions to many bus services, especially the 3 between the Station and the city via the back roads. However, its completion enabled access restrictions to be put in force in Eastgate and Bridge Streets, a bus lane in Bridge Street and then buses only movement at the Cross. These steps made services more reliable and in the first year there was an increase in passenger numbers of some 5%, which by that time was very unusual.

One of the 1972 delivery of Fleetlines, 59, is shown at the Station about to leave for Great Saughall on what was then the 1D service. *(TL/RM)*

The Fleetlines were successful, and another six arrived in 1972. The first three came in February and were similar to the earlier batch, but were of low rather than intermediate height. This was partly to assist the many older people who lived in the city, by making access easier, and partly pragmatic, in that reducing the height meant that there were fewer collisions with overhanging branches on the more rural sections of the network.

The other three arrived in July 1972; there had been criticism of the lack of luggage capacity on the Fleetlines which were already in service and the capacity of the new vehicles was reduced to 72 and space was provided over the nearside wheel arch to house suitcases and the like. All the earlier Fleetlines were rebuilt in 1977/8 so that they too afforded this space.

As the Fleetlines arrived, the older Guy Arabs were gradually withdrawn, but much of the fleet was still of that manufacture. As early as October 1972 it was recorded that 26.5% of the mileage was being run with one-man buses.

In January 1973 the question of providing a local bus exchange point was raised. The turning of vehicles in Town Hall Square was somewhat unsightly, although convenient. There were four proposals for this: the first was on the upper level of a car park in Trinity Street, off Watergate Street, which had been intended for coaches; the second was near Delamere Street, for easy connection with Crosville; the third was in the Frodsham Street area, convenient for many shops; the fourth was between Hunter and Princess Streets, or in other words immediately behind the Town Hall.

The fourth was recommended but the sclerotic pace of local government meant that it was a very long time before that objective was reached.

In June 1973 Hooley indicated that he was intending to retire the following year.

In September 1973 the old-established Trooper Inn terminus, which required the use of the frontage of the very large pub, had to be vacated, at relatively short notice. It had the twin disadvantages of requiring reversing off the main road and also of allegedly damaging the forecourt. Some journeys were cut back to Belgrave Road, but then turned at the Ring Road roundabout, although carrying "Heath Lane" on their destination screens. The service on the 3 and 4 to Christleton Village was enhanced, but this, of course, meant there was an urgent need for extra single-deckers, as the canal bridge on the road to the village had never been rebuilt.

In the very short term, a Leyland Olympian single-decker which had been owned by Fishwicks in Leyland and was still in their livery, was hired from Hollis of Queensferry. In December 1973 two former North Western Road Car AEC Reliances with Willowbrook bodies, dating from 1961, were purchased from SELNEC, which had taken over many of North Western's vehicles and services. They had never been repainted and indeed one was put in service by Chester still in red livery but with Chester fleetnames. It took until 5 October 1974 before a new turning point was constructed on Whitchurch Road, which was very near the Trooper and was thereafter designated as "Canal Bridge", which was not very helpful as a destination to strangers.

The shortage of suitable vehicles in 1973 prompted the purchase of two ex-North Western Willowbrook-bodied AEC Reliances. 65 is seen in the garage, with tramrails still beneath it. *(TL/RM)*

An offside view of 65, also in the garage. *(OS)*

The livery was revised in its application in 1973, although the maroon and ivory were retained. Initially double-deckers were painted with maroon roof and lower-deck panels and with ivory between, but shortly afterwards this was modified and the maroon was carried down to the waist of the upper deck. Single-deckers were largely maroon but with a maroon roof and skirt.

Guy were pleased to be able to announce that they were supplying Arabs with forward-entrance bodywork, and one – in later livery - is seen right, outside Chester Town Hall. One of Crosville's infamous Seddon single-deckers is seen behind in the days when chassis and engine were still together – before the latter were removed after the Seddons were withdrawn, to replace the units in Leyland Nationals. *(Both Massey/STA)*

One of the three Chester Corporation dual-entrance Leyland Tiger Cub PSUC1/11s seen here on 30 July 1977. Number 52 dates from 1966 and clearly shows the large destination displays favoured by this operator. Notice also the flap for the 'Pay as You Enter' sign, open in this instance but closed when a conductor was being carried.

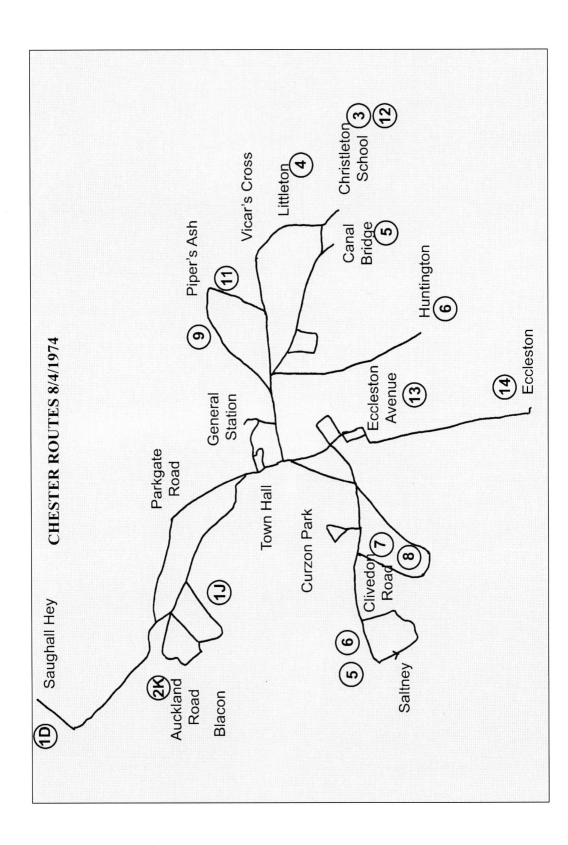

CHESTER ROUTES 8/4/1974

8: BUS OPERATION 1974-85

The Local Government Act 1972 came into force with effect from 1 April 1974. It had less effect on transport in Chester than it had in some other authorities, for many of them were absorbed or amalgamated. It did, however, have profound effects on the administration of the city. Reference has already been made to the constrained local authority boundary, and by this time suburban growth had occurred on all sides. The 1972 Act dispensed completely with all County Boroughs, so Chester became a District, but retained the ability to call itself a City. More importantly it was united with the former Rural Districts of Chester and of Tarvin. This added to the new District a substantial rural area, but it also meant that for the first time the entire Chester suburban area, save only for that in Saltney, which was over the boundary with Wales, was within the same local authority and was thus largely served by vehicles from its own local authority.

The 1974 changes also meant the end of the traditional Chester County Borough FM registration numbers, which had carried by all of the fleet up to that time save those which had been bought second-hand.

Hooley retired on 30 June 1974, thus just after the change in administration, having served almost 20 years in post.

Just before the end of the County Borough Council, its final three vehicles arrived. They were another three Daimler Fleetlines with 72-seat Northern Counties bodies, as had been the last order.

The new administration continued very much along the same lines as the old. The first revisions of services, which took place with effect from 8 April 1974, only a week after the new District took over, but had, of course, been planned before, were wholly positive. The Blacon services 1A, 1B and 2C were incorporated into the pattern of the 1J and 2K, which before then had operated only in evenings, on Sundays, and occasionally at other times. This meant that travellers had a much more predictable service and one which also provided many links around what had become a very well-populated area. Because the 2K absorbed the former 2C, it continued to operate via Highfield Road, Oakfield Road, Melbourne Road and Auckland Road, and after reaching Western Avenue continued back to town via Blacon Point Road and Saughall Road. The roads around Oakfield Road were thus served only on the anti-clockwise circle, whereas the clockwise 1J ran along Blacon Point Road and then straight up Western Avenue. Thus, for the first time Blacon was given not only a frequent and comprehensive service, but one which linked the various parts of the widespread estate and gave connections from all of it to town. It was the vindication of the decision to build the new bridge on Blacon Avenue, over the canal, which had been delayed for so long. The rather odd suffix letters were, of course, a relic of the past, and were no longer needed by this time.

There was another complication with the services to Blacon. Work was carried out in Chichester Street, so a temporary diversion via Garden Lane (the original route) was used instead of Chichester or Walpole and Bouverie Streets. The undertaking decided that that was a preferable way to reach Saughall Road, and applied to the Traffic Commissioners to do so on a permanent basis, but permission was refused; the truth is that all the streets through which the buses had to pass to reach the Saughall Road canal bridge were unsuitable for an intensive service of large vehicles.

At the same time, a similar remedy was applied in Saltney. Instead of terminating at a variety of places in the village, the 5 and 6 were formed into a unidirectional anti-clockwise loop, via High Street, Sandy Lane (the former Ring Road), Boundary Lane, Victoria Road, Irving's Crescent and Park Avenue back to High Street. Some in the Sandy Lane area, which was being developed at this time with privately occupied homes, complained on the grounds of safety, but those in the council houses in Victoria Road thought that the new service pattern was a huge improvement. It also eliminated the confusing multiple destinations, and removed the need for the West View turning point.

An alteration was also made at this time to the 3 service, which had always been something of a Cinderella. It continued to operate from the General Station to Christleton School, but on leaving the Station it travelled a short distance down City Road then cut through behind the garage, via Francis Street, to reach its traditional route of St Anne Street, which was still not producing many passengers. It also had its frequency improved back to a regular hourly all day, which was a great improvement. It was thought that by running from the Station in that direction it would gain traffic, because it would leave from the stances outside the Queen Hotel, as did the other services running into the city centre.

Another suggestion was for an experimental service of four journeys a day to Westminster Park, between Hough Green and Lache Lane. This is unlikely to have attracted much traffic and in any event was never instituted.

The Council also looked to improve its provision for schools. In 1974 a service was introduced to Overleigh Middle School, using some roads not otherwise served. As already mentioned, for some years services (nominally numbered 15) had run from the Station to Chester's leading private school, King's, which was rather outside the built-up area at that time and not on any regular local route.

On 4 February 1974, and thus still under the City Council, it was agreed that three Leyland Leopards with bodies by Northern Counties should be ordered and that an already existing order for three Fleetlines should be increased to five, and that tenders be invited for a further five for 1976/7. Chester was having to pay the delayed price for its long period of ultra-conservatism, which, of course, had made it very popular with the bus enthusiast fraternity.

67, a 1975 Leyland Leopard with Northern Counties body, loads in front of the characteristic Rows before moving on to Eccleston. *(TL/RM)*

68 was also delivered in 1975 and this nearside view shows it on the 12 to Vicar's Cross. *(OS)*

Hooley's replacement was Mr W David Clark. The pressing task which faced him was the further implementation of one-man operation, which was essential because of rising costs, but was very difficult to effect in Chester because so much of the fleet still consisted of robust but outdated Guy Arabs which could not be used in that way. Passenger numbers were reasonably steady at this time at about 9,000,000 to 10,000,000 a year, not least because of the building of so many houses in the area. Like his predecessor, Mr Clark was to remain in post until his retirement, in his case in 1998, well after deregulation and thus beyond the time dealt with by this book. He was clearly interested in the history of the undertaking and, as already mentioned, co-authored a book on the subject. When it was published, by the Manchester Transport Museum Society in 1979, to commemorate the centenary of the horse trams, Chester subsidised it.

A new initiative, which began on 20 May 1974 but lasted initially only until 5 October of that year, was the provision of an experimental shopping service in the inner area. It commenced at Little Roodee car park, near the Castle, and ran via the Cross and the Town Hall to Delamere Street, the Crosville bus station for out-of-town services, and then returned. The vehicle nearly always used for this was an early battery electric vehicle which was hired for the purpose from the Department of Trade and Industry. The service was not remunerative but did show a demand among some, particularly those with restricted ability to walk. The County Council then said it would pay half the deficit on the service so it was continued throughout October and November, save on Wednesday, which was early closing day.

The Council was also still anxious to improve and increase its restricted but conveniently placed garage. In 1974 an adjoining former ambulance depot was acquired and was converted into a body shop with facilities for electricians and also those involved in trimming upholstery.

The Council had set its sights upon the Fleetline as the way forward, but this path was disrupted by the development of the bus production industry. Daimler was purchased by Jaguar in 1960, as was Guy the following year. In 1966 Jaguar merged with the British Motor Holdings and in 1968 that organisation merged with Leyland to form the British Leyland Motor Corporation. In 1973 it

TRAMS AND BUSES OF THE CITY OF CHESTER

W.D. CLARK AND H.G. DIBDIN

was decided to move production of the Fleetline from the traditional Daimler base in Coventry to Leyland. This led to massive delays in the delivery of new vehicles, sometimes up to two years, and it had a particularly adverse effect on Chester because of its need to replace old stock with some urgency.

In 1974 quotes were given by Ailsa, which hoped to benefit from the problems which the BLMC conglomerate were having. The Ailsa was a modern front-engined double-decker, which may have appealed to Chester because of the conservative outlook which permeated the Transport Department. However, on 21 October 1974 it was decided that none should be purchased until they had been proved in service elsewhere; none were in the event ever purchased.

The decision was taken to bridge the gap before Fleetlines could be delivered by replacing some of the older vehicles with single-deckers, which were also seen as of more use for private hire and the like, in which Clark was interested as a way forward. In consequence of this decision, three Leyland Leopards with 47-seat Northern Counties bodies arrived in May and June 1975 and then, because of continuing delays, a further three were ordered and arrived in January 1976. The latter batch held only 43 and were fitted with moquette seating, which was then adopted as standard; its use was intended to make the vehicles more appealing to those wanting to hire them.

These arrivals permitted the replacement of the second hand ex-SELNEC Reliances, but at the beginning of 1974 there were still five Guy Arabs of 1954, two of 1955 and four of 1957 in the fleet.

Not surprisingly with all these problems, there was not much development of the route network in 1975. A city shopper service was reintroduced, but this year it was operated by conventional single-deckers. It ran on a modified route, still starting from Little Roodee, but after the Cross serving the Gorse Stacks car park, then Delamere Street, the Town Hall, the Cross and back to the starting point. It lasted only from 16 June to 13 September of that year. The County Council paid for this.

A classic Chester view of the bridge and clock in Eastgate Street; 70, another Leyland Leopard with Northern Counties body, delivered in 1976, is bound for Christleton via Vicar's Cross on the extended service 12. *(TL/HH)*

In contradistinction to all these problems, private hire was indeed beginning to take off, for double- as well as single-deckers. There was also a great deal of school work, which came to a peak at this time, but was by its nature not very economical because it involved the use of staff and vehicles only for two short periods a day and then only in term-time.

There was an illuminating vignette on 13 October 1975. Crosville invited the committee to view a film which the company had made about the acute financial difficulties which they were suffering. The committee declined. Old conflicts lasted, but soon the time would come when they had to be addressed more constructively.

After the Leopards with Northern Counties bodies had been delivered, Chester decided to order a further six single-deckers. These were again Leyland Leopards, but on this occasion with Duple Dominant bodies, seating 47. They arrived in December 1976. One of them (80) was later painted in two shades of blue and fitted with new seats, to make it more appealing for private hire.

As well as these new vehicles, it was decided during the year that more second-hand buses should be purchased, in order to deal with the crisis which was manifesting itself and was becoming more acute. The Council bought three Leyland Tiger Cubs with 43-seat East Lancs bodies, which had been supplied to Lancaster Corporation in

77 was a Duple-bodied Leopard bought in 1976 and seen on the 4 to Curzon Park with an unusually heavy load of passengers. *(TL/RM)*

80, a similar Duple-bodied Leopard, was repainted in two shades of blue and cream to make it more attractive for private hire. *(TL/RM)*

The purchase from Lancaster of three Leyland Leopards with East Lancs bodies in 1976 was a short-term move. 76 is seen inward bound. *(TL/RM)*

1958/9 and had then passed to Lancaster District Council in 1974 when their former fleet was merged with that of Morecambe & Heysham. One of these elderly vehicles was run in Chester still in blue Lancaster livery and they were a very short-term buy. They arrived in July 1976 and all three had been withdrawn by mid-1977. The total cost of the three was £1,200.

There was, however, another move forward with the network in 1976. With effect from 14 June 1976 the Piper's Ash circular, fractured some 20 years before, was restored, albeit now running along a short portion of the Ring Road (A41) rather than Hare Lane. Services were denoted as 10 via Green Lane and 11 via Hoole Lane: the re-establishment of the circle meant that a number of inter-suburban links were made again. However, the documentation reveals that one of the reasons for this revival was the acute difficulty with turning on Green Lane. As buses became larger and were operated by only one man, and as traffic grew, the need for better facilities for turning at termini became more acute.

Another extension at this time was that many of the 12 journeys to Vicar's Cross, which had terminated in Littleton Lane, were extended the short distance into Littleton, which thus had the best service it had enjoyed since the short period just before the War.

The new single-deckers had tided over the immediate lack of suitable vehicles, but the Council still needed double-deckers, particularly for the heavily-patronised Blacon services.

Thus it was, that in February 1977 three more Fleetlines (this time Leyland Fleetlines, since they were made in Lancashire), with Northern Counties 72-seat bodies came to Chester. It is another measure of the convoluted way in which this and other local authorities operated that, as long before as 23 June 1975, the committee dealing with transport had recommended luxury seating be provided in one of the three, and semi-luxury seating on the other two. This was based on a strong recommendation from Clark that this would assist with private hire. However, the full Council then referred the issue to the policy and resources committee (which did not generally deal with transport) and it was not acted upon.

A year later saw the arrival of a further five Fleetlines, and February 1979 yet another five. The final batch of such vehicles was another five in March 1980. The Fleetlines meant that many of the Guy Arabs were withdrawn, although six were still in the active fleet during 1981. All these double-deckers after 1977 were delivered equipped for one man operation. In many ways Chester was a good example of a place where

81 marked the return of double-deckers in 1977: it was a Leyland Fleetline with Northern Counties body, waiting at the Station for a trip to Saughall on the 1D. *(TL/RM)*

91 was one of the 1979 Fleetlines with Northern Counties bodies, seen on the Station to Saltney circular 16, in Lower Bridge Street. *(TL/RM)*

this could be instituted, because its routes were relatively short. The problems were caused by what had happened before. Also, although the city prided itself on its cheap fares, which it said were the lowest in the North West, here as in other places the use of pre-payment systems and the like lagged behind and did not become common until many years later.

The chronic traffic congestion in the centre of Chester had been much improved by the opening of the Inner Ring Road and the consequent restrictions on access to the centre. It was improved yet further in 1976 when the southern by-pass was opened in December, which took the heavy holiday traffic for North Wales out of the centre of the city.

The Manager was asked in 1979 about operating a minibus service around the area which had been largely pedestrianised, but thought it would not be satisfactory and would impact adversely on the other bus services which the Council was running. Further pedestrianisation took effect from 1 March 1981 and made the city centre much more pleasant for shoppers and visitors alike.

On 28 March 1978 a new unnumbered workers' journey was introduced. It ran from the Town Hall, via Parkgate Road, right round the Blacon Estate, and back towards town on Saughall Road. However, it then turned south down Stadium Way and along Sealand Road into the Stadium Industrial Estate, built around the then home of Chester City FC; a number of industries were being established there and the service enabled those living in Blacon to get there more easily. It was another incursion into an area which was given to Crosville in 1932, but by this time Crosville was not in expansive mood.

There was a more important change with effect from 10 July 1978 when cross-town operation on the 5/6 was abandoned during the daytime period on weekdays. Instead, the 5 ran from Town Hall to the Canal Bridge terminus on Whitchurch Road and the 6 to Huntington (Rake & Pikel). A new service, numbered 16, ran from the Station via the city to Saltney, where it ran round the circle. At non-peak times, the previous regime continued.

With effect from the same date, a new service 2F replaced half the journeys on the 2K; these journeys ran via Western Avenue and the whole length of Melbourne Road to Auckland Road, instead of via Highfield Road, Oakfield Road and Onslow Road on to the very end of Melbourne Road, as did the 2K. These journeys were still unidirectional.

By this time, school services were being given their own numbers. With effect from 5 September 1978 a new service (18) began which was disconnected from the rest of the network and was wholly within Wales. It ran from Broughton (Mold Road) via the British Aerospace Factory and on to St David's School in Saltney, which was further out than had been reached by Chester buses. At the same time, a new school service 19 was introduced from Huntington to Christleton High School, which avoided the necessity for pupils at the latter to change buses.

While many of the services were struggling, particularly those in areas where the houses were well-spaced out, Blacon continued to demand more resources. From 17 November 1980 there was an additional half hourly service from the Station to the Blacon area. Then on 19 January 1981 it was agreed that every half hour a bus to or from Blacon should run via Stadium Way, Whipcord Lane and Raymond Street, an area which had not been served for many years.

The decline in services to more affluent areas was well demonstrated by the further deterioration in the number of buses to Eccleston Avenue. For a time, return journeys ran once again via Eaton Road instead of Eaton Avenue, although they still ran along Appleyards Lane. Then they were restored to Eaton Avenue, but in the evenings and on Sundays the area was served by deviating services to Saltney via Appleyards Lane.

Despite all these matters, the financial position was deteriorating and by January 1981 substantial deficits were being incurred: although the fares remained low, there were frequent applications for increases. On 16 March 1981 the General Manager said that he thought that because of the financial position, only three vehicles a year instead of four should be purchased in each of the next two years.

There was a trivial but psychologically important development with effect from 26 May 1980. The point has already been made that one of the effects of the 1932 agreement was that Chester was unable to run through services from the suburbs to the famous Zoo, which was then outside the city boundary but was now within the new District boundary. Crosville agreed at this time that Chester could run services from the Blacon estate to the Zoo. They ran from the corner of Blacon Avenue and Ludlow Road and were numbered 25. The service ran only in school holiday times.

That minor variation of the 1932 agreement was a prelude to the complete replacement of what had long been an outdated set of terms; it was possible to reach terms, however, only because Crosville's position at this time was much weakened by its widespread financial difficulties and the burden of its many unremunerative country services.

A general agreement between Chester and Crosville was concluded on 22 April 1981, and this was completed by a formal accord signed on 19 July 1981. The main points in this were:

- There was agreement in principle that services and fares should be rationalised;
- All picking up restrictions within the urban area were abolished and Crosville were to apply the low Chester fares in it;
- Crosville service C75 to Waverton was replaced by an extension of Chester service 12, which was thereafter to run Chester-Vicar's Cross-Littleton-Christleton-Brown Heath-Waverton Village and Church, covering new ground for the Corporation after Christleton, albeit within the new District;
- Some Crosville journeys on the C66 to King's School and the C64/65 to Hargrave and Tattenhall, just beyond Waverton, should be transferred to Chester;
- Crosville agreed that Chester should be permitted to continue running along Whipcord Lane and should also be able to continue what became the 23 to the Zoo, from Blacon via the city and the Station.

It is apparent that this concord reflected a change of attitude by both parties, no doubt because it had been forced on them by economic reality. There was undoubtedly pressure also from Cheshire County Council, which wanted the abolition of all restrictive agreements between the undertakings. Some on the Chester side wanted to go further than the agreement which had been reached and to gain access to the Hoole area, from which they had been excluded for so long. However, even under the more liberal provisions of the Transport Act 1980, which reversed the burden of proof in licensing applications for stage carriage services so that the onus was on an objector to show that they should not be granted, Chester would have been very unlikely to have been granted such services by the Traffic Commissioners. Crosville was serving the area with a frequent network, and the routes there were no doubt among their more lucrative.

Waverton was within the new Chester District, but in any event the requirement to obtain the consent of the Traffic Commissioners to operate out of area under s101 of the 1930 Act had been removed by the Transport Act 1968.

At the same time as these important developments were taking place, notice to quit was served on the Post Office in April 1981 in order to obtain possession of land which had been used by it for workshops and had at one time had on it a railway wagon repair works and was now required for the maintenance of the fleet. The new workshops were not ready until May 1983 and an open day and rally was held to mark their opening. It was a further stage in the piecemeal redevelopment of the site.

In 1981 also, Clark introduced an afternoon tour of the city, using one of the newer double-deckers equipped with a public address system. It took in the central area with its many monuments and its views of the Rows and the wall, and also included afternoon tea at Christleton. It was a forerunner of the many such tours which were run in later years, mostly after deregulation.

The Zoo service continued after the agreement with Crosville, albeit only running non-stop from the Station. 1 (RFM 641) was delivered in June 1953 and was one of the Arab IVs with Massey 56-seat body. From January 1976, when it had already run almost 20 years in service, it became a driver training vehicle. It ceased being so used in July 1981 but the next month was reinstated as a PSV and was used on promotional work, and on the special service to Chester Zoo. It was later preserved and recently appeared in restored condition at the Chester-Wrexham Running Day on New Year's Day 2022. It was in the dignified and appropriate pre-1973 livery.

By this time the remaining Arabs were being utilised as an attraction to those who like buses. Leaflets were issued indicating when they were intended to be used, both on the Zoo service and on certain journeys to the east of the city, mainly on services to the Piper's Ash district on Saturdays. 1 and 23, an Arab V with Massey forward entrance body, were generally used. Apart from 1, many of the other Guy Arabs have been preserved, including at least 35 and 36 (FTM 135/6C) of 1965, 42 (XFM 42G) of 1969, and 47 (DFM 347H), the last-numbered of the final delivery, although it is not clear whether it actually arrived after the other two, which would have made it definitively the last Guy. Clark was asked about this and was not sure.

The reinstatement of the Piper's Ash circle had not been entirely successful and there was competition from Crosville, which ran its C36 and 37 circular services to Piper's Ash out via Hoole Road and in via Canadian Avenue and vice versa. With effect from March 1982 a very strange scheme was put in place by Chester. This involved service 9 running to and from Piper's

Ash via Hoole Lane. Service 10 ran to Piper's Ash via Green Lane and returned via Hoole Lane and was unidirectional, so there were more buses back into Chester along Hoole Lane than there were out via the same route. Service 11 ran along Vicar's Cross Road, turned left along the Ring Road, and then returned to town via Green Lane. It too was unidirectional, so a passenger from the former Queen's Road terminus went into town on an 11 and returned on a 10.

The service via Newtown was improved (again) for a time before finally being abandoned, and there was a bus hourly from the Station to Christleton on what became renumbered as the 4: the service to Christleton was supplemented by the extended service 12 to Waverton. On 30 May 1982 Chester resumed Sunday services to Waverton, after a gap of some years. Curzon Park was still on the network, on the grounds of utility to those elderly people who lived there rather than on economic grounds, but now ran from the city only and was numbered 17.

In late 1982 there were grave problems over running along Beckett's Lane, which by then was served by the 5. A petition was raised against rerouting the service via the main road, but a solution was reached by the simple expedient of banning parking on the narrow area where the problems had arisen.

The requirement to purchase double-deckers was still continuing, but in 1981 Chester took a new step. It followed a number of other operators in moving to the Dennis Dominator, although these carried 72-seat bodies by Northern Counties as had the Fleetlines. Chester purchased 14 double-deck Dominators at this time, five in 1981, six in two batches of three in 1982 and a further three in 1983. The move to Dominators was brought about because many undertakings thought that British Leyland was too strong and too self-satisfied, dictating to customers rather than accommodating their specific needs. Chester was to become a haven for many second-hand Dennises after the successor company took over from the City Council in 1986, but also then bought a large number of Dennis Dart single-deckers and some Javelin underfloor-engined coaches. It then became a Dennis rather than a Guy centre.

The Town Hall Square had always been an important centre for local transport and it was much more central than Crosville's country bus station in Delamere Street. One of the restrictions placed on traffic after the construction of the Inner Ring Road was one preventing cars from crossing the Square. However, the stances became congested as the buses which used it increased in size and some thought that they detracted from the streetscape. As already set out, the proposal to replace it as the central terminal had been in gestation for many years. It was not until 1982/3 that the new bus station was constructed behind the Town Hall, which became the centre for the City's services. It was known as the Bus Exchange, which distinguished it clearly from the Crosville Bus Station and in many ways it was an improvement for local passengers, although the vehicles were not immediately visible in the way that they had been. Chester was not the only operator permitted to use the new facility.

Park and Ride schemes are now found in many parts of the United Kingdom: Chester, with its particular problems of congestion and access, was one of the first places in which such a project was introduced. It was initially raised in 1982, and then on 17 November 1983 it began operation from a site leased from Sainsbury's, off Caldy Valley Road in Boughton Heath. It ran from Monday to Saturday until January 1984 and thereafter on Saturdays only, and the buses for it were provided by the City Council. The central terminal was in Frodsham Street.

The scheme was successful and by as early as the summer of 1984 it was resolved to make the service daily for the summer and the Christmas seasons. The continued use made of it meant that in 1985 it was decided to make this site arrangement permanent and to open other such parking places. The next location was on Sealand Road but it did not open until after deregulation: it was initially operated by Crosville, but later by the Council. In due course four sites were established, including a custom-built area at Boughton Heath. On 17 March 1986 it was agreed that the local authority would acquire 2½ acres adjacent to Sainsbury's and that company agreed to lease the land which had been used for another 10 years; the initial lease had expired in January 1985. The scheme was underwritten by the County Council, which met the deficit.

The rebodying of vehicles had once been a very common practice across the country,

Chester became a devotee of the Dennis Dominator after it moved away from Fleetlines. 102 came in 1981 and is seen here on rail replacement duties with vehicles from a variety of operators. *(TL/RM)*

particularly in dealing with vehicles which had been constructed during the war and immediately afterwards, in which unseasoned wood had been used. Chester itself had, of course, done this with a small number of vehicles. By the 1980s, however, this was a very unusual course. In 1983 the General Manager said that one method of saving money was to rebody the three 1972 Fleetlines 55 to 57, OFM 955-7K, rather than buying replacements. The cost of new buses was increasing rapidly at this time and Clark told the committee that a new double-decker would cost some £61,000, whereas a rebody would cost about half of that. The scheme was also consequent upon being able to use the new workshops, and upon having a skilled fitter who could supervise the removal of the original body in house. It was decided, sensibly, to try this with one vehicle and then to take a view about the other two. Thus 57 had its body removed and a new Northern Counties body was fitted. On 5 December 1983 Clark reported to the committee that this had been entirely satisfactory and recommended that the other two be treated in the same way. However, this was never, in fact, done, because the fitter who could carry out the skilled work required left Chester's employment. 57 thus remained unique.

Another aspect of the undertaking at this time was the continued growth of private hire, one of the intentions of which was to make more intensive use of vehicles which were used for school services but otherwise ran little in revenue-earning service. In 1985 the Council eschewed Dennis for new double-deckers and took delivery of four Leyland Olympians. They restarted the fleet numbering system again at 1: the first two were unusual vehicles for a municipal undertaking, particularly one with the conservative tradition which Chester had. These Olympians had Northern Counties coach bodies, seating 73, and were primarily initially used for private hire and on park and ride services. They were named "Chester Express" and "Chester Mail" respectively. The other Olympians had more conventional bus bodies seating 75.

Also in 1985, the Council purchased three Dennis Dominators with Marshall 50-seat bodies from Merthyr Tydfil Transport, which had purchased them new in 1979. It may be thought that eyebrows would have been raised by the sale of these vehicles after only six years, especially as Merthyr had notoriously difficult operating conditions. They had a relatively short period of service in Chester, as could have been predicted, because while they were in South Wales they had had problems both mechanically and with the bodywork. In return, Chester transferred to Merthyr three of their older but more reliable Leyland Leopards with Duple bodies. This was one occasion when

The first two double-deck coaches to be owned were delivered in 1985. 2 (the third vehicle to bear that number) is on the tour, one of the duties for which they were purchased. *(TL/RM)*

The least successful purchase of second-hand vehicles by Chester was that of three single-deck Dennis Dominators with Marshall bodies, which came from Merthyr in 1985. 115 is seen in the Bus Exchange about to leave for Cliveden Road. *(TL/RM)*

Merthyr got the better of the dealings, which was not a pattern often found in their history. Clark had told the committee that the exchange would assist with the interavailability of spare parts and would cost Chester nothing, but it turned out not to be a wise move.

The timetable issued in late 1983 included services run both by Chester and by Crosville, another innovation. By that time the sensible step had been taken of dropping the cumbersome and now unnecessary suffix letters J and K on the Blacon circulars. The clockwise circular became the 1, the anti-clockwise the 2, but those serving Highfield and Oakfield Roads were designated 2A. Those serving Whipcord Lane became 1E or 2E

as the case may be. The journeys to Saughall were numbered separately as 15, and were extended further to Lodge Lane corner, which had always been served by Crosville services via Parkgate Road. By that time some journeys to Christleton direct (4) ran on to Waverton and Hargrave and the services to Whitchurch Road (Canal Bridge) (5) ran via Beckett's Lane.

The last timetable issued on behalf of the municipal undertaking was dated 1 June 1985. It reflected the continued decline in some services from the peak of the post-war period.

The services being run at that time were as follows, with the central terminal being the Bus Exchange:

1. Bus Exchange-Blacon circular (clockwise) (every 15 minutes: of these a bus ran every 30 minutes as 1E via Whipcord Lane).

2. Bus Exchange-Blacon circular via Auckland Road (anti-clockwise) (every 15 minutes, of these a bus ran every 30 minutes as 2E via Whipcord Lane and every 30 minutes via Highfield and Oakfield Roads as 2A).

4. Bus Exchange-Christleton Village direct, with extensions to Hargarve and Tattenhall (every 30 minutes).

5. Bus Exchange-Whitchurch Road (Canal Bridge) via Beckett's Lane (every 30 minutes).

6. Bus Exchange-Huntington (every 30 minutes).

7/8. Bus Exchange-Cliveden Road circular, (every 30 minutes in each direction).

9. Bus Exchange-Hoole Lane-Piper's Ash (every 30 minutes).

10. Bus Exchange-Green Lane-Piper's Ash-Hoole Lane-Bus Exchange (every 30 to 60 minutes) (unidirectional).

11. Bus Exchange-Vicar's Cross-Green Lane-Bus Exchange (every 30 to 60 minutes) (unidirectional).

12. Bus Exchange-Vicar's Cross-Littleton-Christleton-Waverton, with extensions as 4, (hourly).

13. Station-Bus Exchange-Eccleston Avenue (much reduced service).

14. Bus Exchange-Eccleston Avenue-Eccleston (occasional journeys, two via Queen's Park);

15. Station-Bus Exchange-Blacon-Saughall (half hourly to hourly).

16. Station-Bus Exchange-Saltney circular (every 30 minutes).

17. Bus Exchange-Curzon Park, via Appleyards Lane (hourly).

23. Station-Zoo express (school holidays only).

The reduction in services to Saltney was particularly marked: it was not long before that West View had a bus every five minutes.

The four Olympians and three second hand Dominators were not the last vehicles purchased by the municipal undertaking. The final vehicles were two single-deck Leyland coaches with Duple bodies which came from Greater Manchester Transport in the year leading up to privatisation.

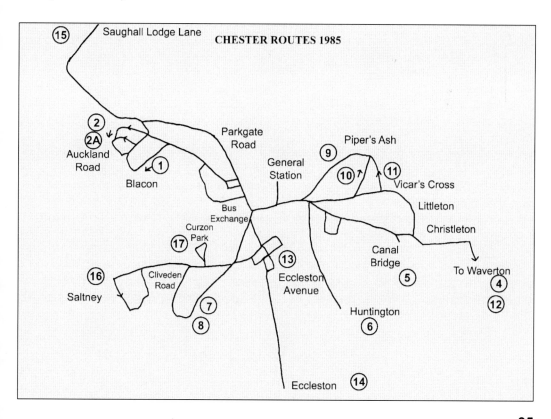

CHESTER ROUTES 1985

9: AFTERMATH

In October 1986 deregulation of bus services meant that Councils were unable thereafter to run undertakings in the traditional way and had to form arm's length companies, which Chester did. It was the end of a small but generally efficient municipal operation which by then had been running since 1902, and buses since 1930. There was a great deal of feeling in the city that local control of bus services should be continued.

The history of the new company is complicated and to include it would have involved doubling the length of this book. It will no doubt deserve a separate study in due course, once more time has passed since the events in question.

David Clark retired in 1998, and was succeeded by Stuart Hyslop.

There was a very large expansion of the fleet, with a great deal of private hire work taken on, and the use of some minibuses.

In 2003 the historic premises near to the Station, which included some of the oldest transport-related buildings in the country, were vacated. The site has been redeveloped and one of the new blocks of flats for students commemorates the previous use: it is known as "Tramways". The site had probably been developed as far as it could, but more space was needed for the larger fleet. New premises were taken on in Bumper's Lane, off Sealand Road, near where a new stadium was built for Chester City FC.

Competition grew; in July 2006 the business was put up for sale, but then in October that year the District Council and the company launched legal proceedings against Arriva PLC and others, alleging that the defendants were exploiting their dominant position in the bus market, contrary to section 18 of the Competition Act 1998. The claim was originally listed for trial on an expedited basis in December 2006, but had to be adjourned because the claimants altered their stance at the last moment. It was then tried in the Chancery Division of the High Court over 12 days in February 2007; judgment was given by Mr Justice Rimer on 15 June 2007.

The action was a disaster for the claimants. The very long judgment gives all sorts of detail about the operation of buses in Chester and in particular confirms that the services to Blacon remained the most profitable. The Judge was critical of some witnesses on both sides (although not of Hyslop) and coruscating about the Council's Strategic Direction officer, who gave evidence on financial matters, but his conclusion was essentially that the expert giving evidence on behalf of the defendants was correct in his view that Arriva did not hold a dominant position in the local market. It was, therefore, inevitable that the claim should be dismissed and that the claimants should pay the very considerable costs. The financial position of the company at the time of the trial was in any event very poor indeed.

The business was then sold to the First Group in the same month that judgment was given, together with 84 vehicles, which shows how much expansion or perhaps over-expansion, had taken place. It was a sad end to the enterprise.

In 2009 Chester became part of the Cheshire West and Chester District, which encompassed a much large population and included other substantial places such as Ellesmere Port.

The present situation in Chester is that the local routes have little relationship with the services which the Council ran. The Blacon circulars are still in operation in recognisable form; the Saltney service has been combined with that to Cliveden Road, but provides a better service to the village than was given by Chester in its last years. The once frequently served Eccleston Avenue area now has only occasional buses heading for villages out of town; there is no service at all to Eccleston Village. The services to the eastern side of the city, which caused so much trouble to the Corporation, have been much reduced. Park & ride has become a very important player in the local economy and the streets around the Cross, which once resounded to the sounds of Fodens and Guy Arabs, are now almost completely pedestrianised.

10: FLEET LIST

FLEET NUMBER	INDEX NUMBER	CHASSIS	BODYWORK

1930

1	FM 5763	AEC Regal	Short B30D
2	FM 5767	AEC Regal	Short B30D
3	FM 5771	AEC Regal	Short B30D
4	FM 5765	AEC Regal	Short B30D
5	FM 5769	AEC Regal	Short B30D
6	FM 5770	AEC Regal	Short B30D
7	FM 5766	AEC Regal	Short B30D
8	FM 5768	AEC Regal	Short B30D
9	FM 5764	AEC Regal	Short B30D
10	FM 5772	AEC Regal	Short B30D
11	FM 5773	AEC Regent	Short H50R
12	FM 5777	AEC Regent	Short H50R
13	FM 5774	AEC Regent	Short H50R
14	FM 5778	AEC Regent	Short H50R
15	FM 5775	AEC Regent	Short H50R
16	FM 5776	AEC Regent	Short H50R
17	FM 6137	AEC Regent	Short H50R
18	FM 6138	AEC Regent	Short H50R
19	FM 6139	AEC Regent	Short H50R
20	FM 6140	AEC Regent	Short H50R

The initial fleet of 20 AEC vehicles lost only two members (16 and 18) before the outbreak of war. Most of the remaining double-deckers were withdrawn in 1943 and the last two (12 and 20) in 1944. In that year, the first four single-deckers were taken out of service and this continued over the next years, with the last (6) remaining in stock until 1949.

1931

21	FM 7045	AEC Regent	Weymann H50R
22	FM 7046	AEC Regent	Weymann H50R

Both these vehicles were withdrawn in 1939, before most of the 1930 deliveries.

1934

23	FM 8649	Bedford WLB	Duple B20F
24	FM 8650	Bedford WLB	Duple B20F
25	FM 8936	Leyland TD3	Massey H52R

The two small Bedfords lasted only until 1939; the first Titan in the fleet was withdrawn in 1945.

1936

26	AFM 517	Leyland TD4c	Massey H52R
27	AFM 518	Leyland TD4c	Massey H52R
28	AFM 519	Leyland TD4c	Massey H52R

All these three Titans were withdrawn in 1945.

1938

29	DFM 390	AEC Regent	East Lancs H54R
30	DFM 391	AEC Regent	East Lancs H54R

These Regents lasted until 1953 in the fleet.

1939

31	DFM 946	AEC Regent	Massey H54R
32	DFM 947	AEC Regent	Massey H54R
33	DFM 948	AEC Regent	Massey H54R
34	DFM 949	AEC Regent	Massey H54R
35	EFM 377	Leyland TD5c	Leyland H53R
36	EFM 378	Leyland TD5c	Leyland H53R

The two 1939 Leylands were withdrawn in 1950. 36 was in due course rebuilt as a coach by Barton. The AECs of the same year went between 1951 and 1953.

1940

37	EFM 909	AEC Regent	Massey H54R
38	EFM 910	AEC Regent	Massey H54R
39	EFM 911	AEC Regent	Massey H54R

This completion of a pre-war order was all disposed of in 1955.

1941

40	FFM 113	Leyland TD7c	Massey H54R
41	FFM 114	Leyland TD7c	Massey H54R
42	FFM 115	Leyland TD7c	Massey H54R

These Leylands, also the completion of a pre-war order, lasted only until 1951.

1942

43	FFM 232	Guy Arab I	Massey H56R
44	FFM 233	Guy Arab I	Massey H56R

The first of many Guys in the fleet had utility bodies and were withdrawn in 1954, after which they were exported to what was then Salisbury, Southern Rhodesia.

1943

45	FFM 270	Daimler CWG5	Massey H56R
46	FFM 278	Guy Arab II	Duple H56R
47	FFM 286	Daimler CWA6	Duple H56R
48	FFM 285	Daimler CWA6	Duple H56R
49	FFM 287	Daimler CWA6	Duple H56R
50	FFM 291	Daimler CWA6	Duple H56R

Of the six further utility vehicles which arrived in 1943, 46 was given a new Massey H56R body in 1953 and lasted until 1969. All the others were not rebodied and were withdrawn between 1954 and 1957.

1944

51	FFM 295	Guy Arab II	Massey H56R
52	FFM 296	Guy Arab II	Massey H56R
53	FFM 297	Guy Arab II	Massey H56R
54	FFM 298	Guy Arab II	Massey H56R
55	FFM 299	Guy Arab II	Massey H56R
56	FFM 321	Daimler CWA6	Brush H56R
57	FFM 322	Daimler CWA6	Brush H56R
58	FFM 323	Daimler CWA6	Brush H56R

Of the eight further utilities delivered in 1944, 53 and 54 were rebodied by DJ Davies with H56R bodies in 1952; in the same year 55 received a new Massey H56R body. The two Davies rebodied vehicles were withdrawn in 1961, the Massey as late as 1968. Those which were not rebodied were withdrawn between 1954 and 1957.

1945

59	FFM 324	Daimler CWA6	Brush H56R

This was the last utility specification vehicle taken into the fleet and was withdrawn in 1961.

1946

64	FFM 660	AEC Regal	Massey B32F
65	FFM 661	AEC Regal	Massey B32F

The first non-utility vehicles for some years had long lives. 64 lasted until 1962 and 65 to 1967.

1947

60	HFM 170	Daimler CVA6	Massey H56R
61	HFM 171	Daimler CVA6	Massey H56R
62	HFM 172	Daimler CWD6	Massey H56R
63	HFM 173	Daimler CWD6	Massey H56R
66	HFM 174	Daimler CWD6	Massey H56R
67	HFM 175	Daimler CVA6	Massey H56R
68	HFM 176	AEC Regal	Massey B32F
69	HFM 177	AEC Regal	Massey B32F

The double-deck deliveries in 1947 were parts of two orders: four Daimlers with Daimler engines were ordered in 1945, three were delivered in 1947 and the remaining one the following year. A further four but with AEC engines were ordered in 1946, and similarly three arrived in 1947 and one the following year. The first Daimler-engined vehicle went as early as 1957, the other two in 1962. The four AEC-engined vehicles lasted until 1963. The two Regals lasted until 1973 and 1967 respectively.

1948

70	HFM 976	Daimler CVA6	Massey H56R
71	HFM 977	Daimler CWD6	Massey H56R
72	JFM 745	Foden PVD6G	Massey H56R

70 and 71 were the remaining vehicles under the orders of 1946 and 1945 respectively. They lasted until 1963 (70) and 1966 (71). The Foden was the first of that marque and been exhibited at the Commercial Motor Show, so had a higher specification of bodywork. It lasted in service until 1965, a good time.

1949

73	JFM 746	Foden PVD6G	Massey H56R
74	JFM 747	Foden PVD6G	Massey H56R
75	JFM 748	Foden PVD6G	Massey H56R
76	JFM 749	Foden PVD6G	Massey H56R

These four Fodens also had long lives. They were not withdrawn until 1965 or 1966: 74 went to Warrington Corporation, the largest municipal operator of the make, for spares.

1950

77	MFM 556	Foden PVD6G	Massey H56R
78	MFM 557	Foden PVD6G	Massey H56R

The 1950 Fodens lasted until 1968 and 1970 respectively.

1951

79	MFM 634	Foden PVD6G	DJ Davies H56R
80	MFM 635	Foden PVD6G	DJ Davies H56R
81	OFM 33	Foden PVD6G	Massey H56R

The Massey-bodied Foden, the last to be delivered, was in service until 1966, a full life. However, the two Davies-bodied vehicles deteriorated rapidly and were withdrawn as early as 1958.

1953

1	RFM 641	Guy Arab IV	Massey H56R
2	RFM 642	Guy Arab IV	Massey H56R
3	RFM 643	Guy Arab IV	Massey H56R

1953 saw the start of the devotion to the Guy Arab which was to mark the Chester fleet for many years. Numbers were recommenced from 1. Vehicle 1 was used as a driver training vehicle from 1976 but has been preserved. 2 lasted until 1972 and 3 to 1973.

1954

4	RFM 644	Guy Arab IV	Guy/Park Royal H56R
5	RFM 645	Guy Arab IV	Guy/Park Royal H56R
6	RFM 646	Guy Arab IV	Guy/Park Royal H56R
7	UFM 858	Guy Arab IV	Massey H56R
8	UFM 859	Guy Arab IV	Massey H56R
9	UFM 860	Guy Arab IV	Massey H56R
10	UFM 861	Guy Arab IV	Massey H56R

These two batches were withdrawn between 1972 and 1975.

1955

11	UFM 862	Guy Arab IV	Massey H56R
12	UFM 863	Guy Arab IV	Massey H56R
13	XFM 521	Guy Arab IV	Massey H58R
14	XFM 522	Guy Arab IV	Massey H58R
15	XFM 523	Guy Arab IV	Massey H58R

16	XFM 524	Guy Arab IV	Massey H58R
17	XFM 525	Guy Arab IV	Massey H58R
18	XFM 526	Guy Arab IV	Massey H58R

The need to modernise the fleet led to a further eight vehicles arriving in 1955. The first two, which had 6-cylinder engines, lasted until 1976: the others, which had the less powerful 5-cylinder engines, were withdrawn in 1970/1.

1957

19	713 CFM	Guy Arab IV	Massey H60R
20	714 CFM	Guy Arab IV	Massey H60R
21	715 CFM	Guy Arab IV	Massey H60R
22	716 CFM	Guy Arab IV	Massey H60R
23	717 CFM	Guy Arab IV	Massey H60R

The 1957 Arabs were withdrawn between 1973 and 1976.

1959, ACQUIRED VEHICLES

| 56 | DTR 907 | Guy Arab II | Park Royal H56R |
| 57 | DTR 911 | Guy Arab II | Park Royal H56R |

These vehicles were new to Southampton Corporation in 1946. They were withdrawn by Chester in 1968/9.

1961

24	324 VFM	Guy Arab IV	Massey H73F
25	325 VFM	Guy Arab IV	Massey H73F
26	326 VFM	Guy Arab IV	Massey H73F

These were the first 30 feet long and the first eight feet wide vehicles owned by Chester. They were withdrawn after 15 years.

1962

27	327 VFM	Guy Arab IV	Massey H73F
28	328 VFM	Guy Arab IV	Massey H73F
29	329 VFM	Guy Arab IV	Massey H73F
30	330 VFM	Guy Arab IV	Massey H73F

The 1962 Arabs were withdrawn between 1975 and 1978.

1963

31	4831 FM	Guy Arab V	Massey H73F
32	4832 FM	Guy Arab V	Massey H73F
33	4833 FM	Guy Arab V	Massey H73F
34	4834 FM	Guy Arab V	Massey H73F

The 1963 delivery of Arabs was withdrawn between 1975 and 1979.

1963 ACQUIRED VEHICLE

| 51 | LTV 700 | AEC Regal III | East Lancs B35R |

This vehicle was new to Nottingham City Transport in 1951. It lasted with Chester until as late as 1970, a very late date for a half cab single-decker in a municipal fleet.

1965

35	FFM 135C	Guy Arab V	Massey H73F
36	FFM 136C	Guy Arab V	Massey H73F
37	FFM 137C	Guy Arab V	Massey H73F
38	FFM 138C	Guy Arab V	Massey H73F

These Arab Vs were withdrawn in 1981/2.

1966

39	LFM 139D	Guy Arab V	Massey H73F
40	LFM 140D	Guy Arab V	Massey H73F
41	LFM 141D	Guy Arab V	Massey H73F
52	LFM 152D	Leyland PSUC1/11	Massey B40D

These Arabs had shorter lives than some, being withdrawn in 1978/9. The Leopard went in 1981.

1967

53	RFM 453F	Leyland PSUC1/11	Massey B40D

This vehicle lasted only until 1978.

1968

54	XFM 54G	Leyland PSUC1/11	Massey B40D

The third of the Leopards lasted until 1981.

1969

42	XFM 42G	Guy Arab V	Northern Counties H73F
43	XFM 43G	Guy Arab V	Northern Counties H73F
44	XFM 44G	Guy Arab V	Northern Counties H73F
45	DFM 345H	Guy Arab V	Northern Counties H73F
46	DFM 346H	Guy Arab V	Northern Counties H73F
47	DFM 347H	Guy Arab V	Northern Counties H73F

The last of the many Guy Arabs in the fleet had shorter lives than some of their predecessors, because of their apparent obsolescence. They were withdrawn between 1979 and 1982.

1970

48	JFM 648J	Daimler CRG6LX	Northern Counties H74F
49	JFM 649J	Daimler CRG6LX	Northern Counties H74F
50	JFM 650J	Daimler CRG6LX	Northern Counties H74F

These were rebuilt to H72F in 1977/8 to give more room for luggage.

1972

55	OFM 955K	Daimler CRG6LX	Northern Counties H74F
56	OFM 956K	Daimler CRG6LX	Northern Counties H74F
57	OFM 957K	Daimler CRG6LX	Northern Counties H74F
58	WFM 158K	Daimler CRG6LX	Northern Counties H72F

59	WFM 159K	Daimler CRG6LX	Northern Counties H72F
60	WFM 160K	Daimler CRG6LX	Northern Counties H72F

55-57 were rebuilt to H72F in 1977/8 to give more room for luggage. 57 was rebodied by Northern Counties with a new H72F body in 1983. 57, 59 and 60 passed to the successor company in 1986; the others were withdrawn in 1985.

1973 ACQUIRED VEHICLES

64	RDB 859	AEC Reliance	Willowbrook B43F
65	RDB 863	AEC Reliance	Willowbrook B43F

These vehicles were new to North Western in 1961 and were acquired from SELNEC (Cheshire). They were withdrawn in 1976.

1974

61	RFM 61M	Daimler CRG6LX	Northern Counties H72F
62	RFM 62M	Daimler CRG6LX	Northern Counties H72F
63	RFM 63M	Daimler CRG6LX	Northern Counties H72F

These all passed to the limited company.

1975

66	HEN 866N	Leyland PSU4C/2R	Northern Counties B47F
67	HEN 867N	Leyland PSU4C/2R	Northern Counties B47F
68	HEN 868N	Leyland PSU4C/2R	Northern Counties B47F

These had a short life and were withdrawn in 1982.

1976

69	NMB 69P	Leyland PSU4C/2R	Northern Counties B43F
70	NMB 70P	Leyland PSU4C/2R	Northern Counties B43F
71	NMB 71P	Leyland PSU4C/2R	Northern Counties B43F
75	TMB 875R	Leyland PSU4D/2R	Duple B47F
76	TMB 876R	Leyland PSU4D/2R	Duple B47F
77	TMB 877R	Leyland PSU4D/2R	Duple B47F
78	TMB 878R	Leyland PSU4D/2R	Duple B47F
79	TMB 879R	Leyland PSU4D/2R	Duple B47F
80	TMB 880R	Leyland PSU4D/2R	Duple B47F

69 and 78 were withdrawn in 1985 and the others went to the limited company. 80 was reseated to DP41F in 1981 for private hire work.

1976 ACQUIRED VEHICLES

72	175 FTJ	Leyland PSUC1/3	East Lancs B43F
73	389 JTD	Leyland PSUC1/3	East Lancs B43F
74	390 JTD	Leyland PSUC1/3	East Lancs B43F

These three vehicles were a short-term purchase to cover a lack of vehicles and were bought from Lancaster City Council. 72 had been new in 1958 and the other two in 1959. They lasted only a short time and all had gone by 1977.

1977

81	VCA 181R	Leyland FE30AGR	Northern Counties H72F
82	VCA 182R	Leyland FE30AGR	Northern Counties H72F
83	VCA 183R	Leyland FE30AGR	Northern Counties H72F

The 1977 arrivals represented a return to double-deckers. They all passed to the limited company.

1978

84	CFM 84S	Leyland FE30AGR	Northern Counties H72F
85	CFM 85S	Leyland FE30AGR	Northern Counties H72F
86	CFM 86S	Leyland FE30AGR	Northern Counties H72F
87	CFM 87S	Leyland FE30AGR	Northern Counties H72F
88	CFM 88S	Leyland FE30AGR	Northern Counties H72F

1979

89	KFM 189T	Leyland FE30AGR	Northern Counties H72F
90	KFM 190T	Leyland FE30AGR	Northern Counties H72F
91	KFM 191T	Leyland FE30AGR	Northern Counties H72F
92	KFM 192T	Leyland FE30AGR	Northern Counties H72F
93	KFM 193T	Leyland FE30AGR	Northern Counties H72F

1980

94	SDM 94V	Leyland FE30AGR	Northern Counties H72F
95	SDM 95V	Leyland FE30AGR	Northern Counties H72F
96	SDM 96V	Leyland FE30AGR	Northern Counties H72F
97	SDM 97V	Leyland FE30AGR	Northern Counties H72F
98	SDM 98V	Leyland FE30AGR	Northern Counties H72F

The 1977 deliveries were replicated in 1978, 1979, and 1980. All these vehicles passed to the limited company in 1986.

1981

99	YMA 99W	Dennis Dominator	Northern Counties H72F
100	YMA 100W	Dennis Dominator	Northern Counties H72F
101	YMA 101W	Dennis Dominator	Northern Counties H72F
102	YMA 102W	Dennis Dominator	Northern Counties H72F
103	YMA 103W	Dennis Dominator	Northern Counties H72F

1981 saw the move to Dennis. All these vehicles went to the limited company.

1982

104	HMA 104X	Dennis Dominator	Northern Counties H72F
105	HMA 105X	Dennis Dominator	Northern Counties H72F
106	HMA 106X	Dennis Dominator	Northern Counties H72F
107	KLG 107Y	Dennis Dominator	Northern Counties H72F
108	KLG 108Y	Dennis Dominator	Northern Counties H72F
109	KLG 109Y	Dennis Dominator	Northern Counties H72F

Another six Dominators followed in 1982 and they too passed to the limited company.

1983

110	A110 UCA	Dennis Dominator	Northern Counties H72F
111	A111 UCA	Dennis Dominator	Northern Counties H72F
112	A112 UCA	Dennis Dominator	Northern Counties H72F

These three Dominators also passed to the limited company.

1985

1	B201 EFM	Leyland ONLXB/1R	Northern Counties CH73F
2	B202 EFM	Leyland ONLXB/1R	Northern Counties CH73F
3	B203 EFM	Leyland ONLXB/1R	Northern Counties H75F
4	B204 EFM	Leyland ONLXB/1R	Northern Counties H75F

In 1985 there was a reversion to Leyland and the first two double-deck coaches to be owned formed the first part of the order. All passed to the limited company.

1985 ACQUIRED VEHICLES

113	CKG 215V	Dennis Dominator	Marshall B50F
114	CKG 216V	Dennis Dominator	Marshall B50F
115	CKG 216V	Dennis Dominator	Marshall B50F

These three single-deck Dominators came from Merthyr Tydfil in exchange for three older Leyland Leopards. They were new to Merthyr in 1979 and were transferred to the limited company in 1986, but had only a short life with it.

1986 ACQUIRED VEHICLES

21	SND 83X	Leyland PSU3B/4R	Duple C51F
22	SND 87X	Leyland PSU3B/4R	Duple C51F

These two coaches came from Greater Manchester Transport and passed to the limited company later in 1986.